ACADEMIC MOBILITY AND INTERNATIONAL ACADEMICS

Surviving and Thriving in Academia provides short, accessible books for navigating the many challenges, responsibilities and opportunities of academic careers. The series is particularly dedicated to supporting the professional journeys of early and mid-career academics and doctoral students but will present books of use to scholars at all stages in their careers. Books within the series draw on real-life examples from international scholars, offering practical advice and a supportive and encouraging tone throughout.

Series Editor: Marian Mahat, The University of Melbourne, Australia

In this series:

Women Thriving in Academia
Edited by Marian Mahat, The University of Melbourne

Achieving Academic Promotion
Edited by Marian Mahat, The University of Melbourne & Jennifer Tatebe, University of Auckland

Getting the Most Out of Your Doctorate: The Importance of Supervision, Networking and Becoming a Global Academic
Edited by Mollie Dollinger, La Trobe University, Australia

Coaching and Mentoring for Academic Development
By Kay Guccione & Steve Hutchinson

Academic Resilience: Personal Stories and Lessons Learnt from the COVID-19 Experience
By Marian Mahat, Joanne Blannin, Elizer Jay de los Reyes, & Caroline Cohrssen

This is such an important book for everyone working in higher education. The personal reflections of international academics around the globe throughout are both thought-provoking and inspiring, providing understanding of the personal journeys of international academics who form part of our diverse academic community.

–Hannah-Louise Holmes, Deputy Faculty Pro-Vice Chancellor Faculty of Business and Law and Dean of the Business School, Manchester Metropolitan University, United Kingdom

A must-read volume that captures the academic journey and contribution of international academics to global higher education! All scholars including faculty, students and administrators will benefit from reading this book.

–Krishna Bista, Professor of Higher Education, Morgan State University, Maryland (USA)

ACADEMIC MOBILITY AND INTERNATIONAL ACADEMICS

Challenges and Opportunities

EDITED BY

JASVIR KAUR NACHATAR SINGH

La Trobe University, Australia

United Kingdom – North America – Japan – India
Malaysia – China

Emerald Publishing Limited
Howard House, Wagon Lane, Bingley BD16 1WA, UK

First edition 2022

British Library Cataloguing in Publication Data
A catalogue record for this book is available from the British Library

ISBN: 978-1-80117-513-5 (Print)
ISBN: 978-1-80117-510-4 (Online)
ISBN: 978-1-80117-512-8 (Epub)

Printed and bound by CPI Group (UK) Ltd, Croydon, CR0 4YY

ISOQAR certified
Management System,
awarded to Emerald
for adherence to
Environmental
standard
ISO 14001:2004.

Certificate Number 1985
ISO 14001

INVESTOR IN PEOPLE

CONTENTS

Section 3 Personal and Family Experiences in Long- and Short-Term Mobilities

ABOUT THE CONTRIBUTORS

Dr James Burford, PhD, is an Assistant Professor in Global Education and International Development at the Department of Education Studies at Warwick University in the UK. Originally from Aotearoa/New Zealand, James has had academic migration experiences in Thailand (2014–2018), Australia (2018–2021), and the UK (2021–). He also has an active interest in both short and longer-term academic mobilities, researching both academic conferences as well as the experiences of aa-jaan dtàang châat [academic migrants] in Thailand. James is the current co-chair of the Academic Mobilities and Immobilities International Network (AMIIN) and co-edits Conference Inference, a blog about academic conferences. James' broader research interests include the academic profession and doctoral education, international higher education, and gender and sexualities in education. He tweets at @jiaburford.

Dr Ariunaa Enkhtur is an Assistant Professor at the Center for Global Initiatives, Osaka University, Japan. She received her PhD in Transformative Education from the Graduate School of Human Sciences, Osaka University, under the Japanese government scholarship, and her Master's degree in Higher Education Administration from Syracuse University, USA, as a Fulbright scholar. Originally from a Mongolian academic family, she always aspired to work in academia but never imagined working abroad. However, her journey for education exposed her to academic work experiences in the US and now Japan. She has a family of four, and her husband is also an early academic in Japan.

Mary Eppolite is an Assistant Lecturer in Humanities and Language at Mahidol University International College in Thailand. She earned her Masters' degree in TESOL from SIT Graduate Institute in the USA. Mary has experience working in English language education in Thailand, Costa Rica, France, and Peru. She is interested in the impact of English hegemony in the classroom and culturally reflexive pedagogies. Mary has co-published work which has appeared in venues such as *Higher Education, Journal of Higher Education Policy and Management and Globalisation, Societies and Education*. Her current research is focused on team teaching in language education contexts.

Dr Sainbayar Gundsambuu is an Instructor of English at the Kyoto University of Foreign Studies, Kyoto, Japan, and Senior Lecturer at the British and American Studies Department, National University of Mongolia, Mongolia He received his PhD in International Education from Osaka University, Japan, and has been teaching in the higher education sector for over 16 years, of which, the last two years were in Japan. His primary research interests focus on the internationalisation of higher education, English-medium instruction, as well as TESOL. Dr Sainbayar was a recipient of the Fulbright Scholarship in 2011.

Dr Jinan Issa is a very enthusiastic and highly motivated university professor with a dedicated passion to conduct research about higher education, TESOL, quality of teaching and learning, and academic acculturation. She completed her

MEd and PhD degrees in Education/TESOL with distinctions from Universiti Sains Malaysia and was awarded the University's Gold Medal for being the most outstanding candidate in education. She also received the university's fellowship scheme and was one of its brilliant student ambassadors. With over 18 years of experience in different countries of the MENA region, Malaysia and Canada, she came across different challenges and was fortunate to obtain exceptional opportunities. She started her career in 1998 as a translator and an interpreter in the Ministry of Industry and Minerals in Baghdad, Iraq. Later, she worked as an ESL instructor and a trainer in Azzawiya Oil Refining Company from 2005 to 2008 when she decided to pursue her postgraduate studies. She gained research skills and was indulged in research culture, which was evidenced in her quality publications in the second semester of her master's study. Her experience as a researcher was enhanced in her PhD journey when she received the exceptional opportunity to work on an international project in four countries: Malaysia, Australia, Hong Kong and South Korea. Later, her job as an Assistant Professor at the Omani University of Applied Sciences and Technology for over 5 years followed by receiving an offer from the APEX university USM to work in the National Higher Education Research Institute (IPPTN) was another unique experience. She immigrated to Canada and started another academic adventure to receive the OCELT recognition from TESL Ontario. She learnt tens of lessons gained from substantial experiences teaching international postgraduates and multicultural undergraduates.

Dr Jisun Jung is an Assistant Professor in the Faculty of Education at the University of Hong Kong. Her current research focuses on academic profession, doctoral education, master's education and employment, and higher education research in Asia. Her recent co-edited books include *The Changing Academic Profession in Hong Kong* (with Gerard A. Postiglione, Springer, 2017) and *Researching Higher Education in Asia: History, Development and Future* (with Hugo Horta and Akiyoshi Yonezawa, Springer, 2018). She is a co-editor of *Higher Education Research & Development.*

Dr Amrita Kaur is an Assistant Professor of Psychology at WenZhou-Kean University in China. Her research interests include teaching, learning and assessment in higher education, students as partners, learning motivation and engagement and cross-cultural studies for learning. She teaches psychology courses to undergraduate students. She serves as the editorial member for Scopus indexed journal – *Malaysian Journal of Learning and Instruction* and *International Journal of Students as Partners.*

Dr Vijay Kumar is an Associate Professor of Higher Education at the Higher Education Development Centre University of Otago, New Zealand. Prior to joining Otago, he served as an Associate Professor of Linguistics in a public university in Malaysia. Vijay's research interests are in doctoral supervision practices, doctoral examination, academic well-being and feedback practices. He is an academic staff developer with expertise in doctoral supervision. His expertise is recognised globally through invitations for capacity building of doctoral supervisors in 23 countries. He is a UK Council of Graduate Education's recognised doctoral supervisor – the first outside the UK.

Dr Shannon Mason is an Assistant Professor in the Faculty of Education at Nagasaki University, Japan. She completed her doctoral research at Griffith University in Australia, but relocated to Japan during the final two years of her candidature to take up an academic position. She has a broad research agenda within education that spans from P-12 to PhD. Her recent and continuing studies are related to higher education focusing on scholarly publishing, research dissemination, peer review and the experiences of mothers in academia. In Japan, she has been interested in supporting researchers to develop their international visibility through online networks.

Dr Muhammad Muftahu is a Nigerian, who works as a Senior Lecturer, Deputy Director and Coordinator of the Global Higher Education Network (GHEN) at the National Higher Education Research Institute, Universiti Sains Malaysia (USM). He is also the Coordinator of the Professional Programme in Higher Education Leadership and Management, Co-Coordinator of Higher Education Access and Success research cluster, and Commission Member of the Academic Talent Management Project (ATM) 2020, Universiti Sains Malaysia. His research interest and expertise include Higher Education Sustainable Leadership and Management, Comparative and International Higher Education, Higher Education and Industry, Higher Education as Field of Study and Qualitative Methodology.

Muhammad has immensely contributed to the development of higher education as a discipline of study and practices through teaching, postgraduate supervision, research, and wide publication, which awarded him with several academic recognitions at home and abroad, including garnering international grants. Similarly, he is a member and a fellow of various higher education professional bodies and networks across the globe, such as the Society for Research into Higher Education (SRHE), United Kingdom, Nigeria Society for Higher Education Research and Development (NSHERD), Higher Education Research Association (HERA), Malaysian Society for Higher Education Policy and Research Development (Pen-DaPat), Nigerian Institute of Management (NIM), and the

Academy of Management Nigeria (AMN). Giving back to the community by promoting higher education research in Nigeria and national development, he founded the Nigerian Society for Higher Education Research and Development (NSHERD), – the first platform of its kind bringing various scholars of interest for researching higher education in Nigeria. Similarly, recognising his contribution earned him to be appointed as Chairman Visitation Panel, Kaduna State University (KASU) for the period of 2016–2020 which he completed with thoroughness and diligence.

Yuhang Rong serves as the Associate Vice President for Global Affairs and Associate Professor in Residence of Educational Leadership at the University of Connecticut (UConn). He represents UConn as its Senior Leader at the global research university consortium, Universitas 21. He oversees the State of Connecticut partnership with the German state of Baden-Wuerttemberg. Concurrently, he is the Vice Chair of the Board of Directors at the Council for the Accreditation of Educator Preparation (CAEP) in Washington, DC; and he is a member of the Advisory Board for the Queen Rania Teacher Academy in Jordan. Yuhang earned his BA in English from East China Normal University (华东师范大学), MA in Education Administration from West Virginia University, and PhD in Professional Higher Education Administration from the University of Connecticut.

Dr Yusuke Sakurai is a Lecturer at Ochanomizu University, Tokyo, Japan. He received a PhD from the University of Helsinki, Finland. His main subjects are teaching and learning in international settings and support for foreign early-career researchers. He has worked in several countries, including Thailand, Australia, Malaysia, Egypt, Finland and Japan. He has written research outputs on students' perceptions and learning in immersion programmes, foreign language classrooms, study abroad experiences, short-term intensive international courses and doctoral programmes as international students.

Dr Jasvir Kaur Nachatar Singh is an award-winning Senior Lecturer at the Department of Management, Sport and Tourism, La Trobe Business School, La Trobe University, Australia. In 2020, Dr Singh received an international teaching recognition from Advance HE, UK, as a Fellow (FHEA). In 2018, Dr Singh received two La Trobe University Teaching Awards and Best Presenter Award at the Global Higher Education Forum, Malaysia. Dr Singh's research expertise is in higher education discipline with a particular interest exploring international students' current issues such as their academic success, lived experiences, employability, career aspirations as well as learning experiences in a blended learning environment. In addition, Dr Singh also explores lived experiences of international academics and recent work is on international academics with leadership positions. Dr Singh has published several articles in high-impact journals and has presented at numerous national and international higher education conferences in Malaysia, Hong Kong, New Zealand, Thailand, Hawaii, Japan and Australia. In 2020, Dr Singh was appointed as the Associate Editor for *Higher Education Research & Development* journal. In 2018, Dr Singh was appointed as a Research Fellow at the Malaysian National Higher Education Research Institute.

Dr Ashleigh-Jane Thompson is a Senior Lecturer and Program Director in the La Trobe Business School, where she is involved with the sport management programme. Throughout her academic career, she has developed and taught a variety of Undergraduate and Masters coursework subjects and has supervised several Masters and PhD students. She is an award-winning researcher whose primary research activities are in the fields of sport communication, sport marketing, fan engagement and sport innovation. Her research has a theoretical and practical impact both nationally and internationally. She is an active researcher within La Trobe's Centre for Sport and Social Impact and collaborates with other researchers within Australia and internationally. Ashleigh-Jane is also currently the Vice-President of the Sport Management Association of Australia and New Zealand (SMAANZ). In addition to her scholarly pursuits, she maintains active connections with the sport industry by partnering with sport organisations for research projects, as well as working in media operations at national and international sporting events and serving as a Director on various sport organisation boards. She also regularly engages with the media as an outlet to translate her research and encourage public dialogue and debate.

PREFACE

The COVID-19 pandemic and its ongoing challenges continue to change academia as we know it. As time passes by, we have discovered that, in the end, what changes take place, when and why depend on the conscious decisions we make as staff members in each of our roles – from our particular vantage point in teaching and learning, research and service – and, most importantly, on our ability to distinguish what is urgent (survival) from our longer time horizons (growing and thriving, as we hope).

This new precarious environment has also brought to the fore academia's most troubling assumptions, some of which were already being defied by a growing consciousness about global and systemic inequalities, and a recognised need to re-orient our livelihoods as a consequence of environmental degradation and climate change. As much as we pride ourselves of being in 'the ivory tower' watching the world at distance and commenting/engaging with it as needed, we are inextricably embedded in that same world. We are affected by it, one way or the other, and our passivity legitimises what is noble and troubling about it. We are called, then, to participate in our own ways in the calls for action, conversations, decisions and new paths ahead that could result from positioning ourselves as agents of change.

I reflect on these overall trends as I read this book and consider the individual experiences that lie at the heart of the editor and authors' work. I am an international academic myself – someone born in another country, who grew up and was educated in another socio-cultural milieu, who navigated unfamiliar and uncertain pathways to study and work overseas, and who serendipitously arrived at the same maze of corridors of La Trobe's beautiful Bundoora Campus in Melbourne. There, I met Dr Jasvir Singh, my colleague and the editor of this volume, alongside other colleagues who had also 'come from away' and hailed from a wide range of backgrounds. Despite the wide diversity of life and professional experiences we embodied and carried, we all acknowledge many things in common with one another as 'international academics'.

Here we are, living and working in a system conditioned, pushed or pulled by 'a variety of structural factors', which means constantly living on the edge in practice – first as students, then as academics; constantly assessing our strengths and limitations, yearning for a sense of stability. Hoping for (and living) career dreams in our respective disciplines and programmes, whilst putting between brackets (and addressing) all sorts of financial and logistical problems and major pending questions – including whether we belong, or not, whether we speak the language, or not, whether we 'mask' successfully in a cultural environment different than ours, or not, whether we are able to survive (or let alone thrive), or not. And so forth. Day by day, often for years, encouraged to think about ourselves as being privy to the wealth of opportunities of global academia, a world where any of those troubling dilemmas often go unrecognised – and hence unaddressed – by institutions and the academic community in a broader sense.

Yet, at the same time that those problems are real and require attention, it behoves us to consider, highlight and celebrate the courage and effort of many international colleagues who – despite being caught in a maze of uncertainty and precarity – are also able to make the most of the opportunities at hand. Thus, the task of evaluation, recognition and critical analysis of the international academic should not only limit itself to denouncing problems but also to recognising accomplishments – as Jasvir Singh correctly points out in the introduction to this volume. That is, approaching the experiences of international academics with nuance and empathy, open to listening without reservations, connecting with what identifies all of us in this ever-changing environment. There is much to learn from the daily experiences of international academics who, like all of us, carry on their lives in an increasingly competitive and precarious academic environment. This was already the case before the pandemic, and it is even more the case nowadays.

As international academics face new barriers and difficulties in this new era – including even more uncertain job prospects, logistic difficulties, forced distancing from colleagues abroad and, more importantly, loved ones, among other challenges – it will be more important than ever to recognise their difficulties, but also their roles and unique contributions to the academic world and our respective institutions. This book is a major step in this direction. It is a must-read book for current and/or future international academics – whether thinking of short- or long-term mobility in academia. My most sincere congratulations to the editor and contributors around the world to this volume. This is one of the strengths of the book, as it draws on varied experiences and voices of international academics, globally. I look forward to the many stimulating conversations it will elicit and, hopefully, the decisions and policies that it will help inspire in the future.

Raúl Sánchez Urribarrí is a Senior Lecturer in Crime, Justice and Legal Studies at the Department of Social Inquiry, La Trobe University. He has served as Coordinator of Short-Term International Mobility at the School of Humanities and Social Sciences. He holds a PhD in Political Science from the University of South Carolina, an LLM from Cambridge University and a Law Degree from Universidad Catolica Andres Bello (Venezuela). His research focuses on democracy and the rule of law, and it has been published in a variety of outlets, including *The Journal of Politics*, *Law & Social Inquiry*, the *Annual Review of Law and Social Sciences* and *International Political Science Review*. He is a Non-Resident Research Fellow at Tulane University's Center for Inter-American Policy and Research, and a Co-Editor at *Thesis Eleven journal*. Currently, he serves as Chair of the Section on Venezuelan Studies (SVS) of the Latin American Studies Association (LASA).

INTRODUCTION

This book was initiated during one of the lockdowns in Melbourne in 2020 due to the COVID-19 pandemic. I emailed Dr Marian Mahat (the series editor of the *Surviving and Thriving in Academia* book series) after reading her edited book titled 'Achieving Academic Promotion' to just let her know that her chapter on promotion has helped me to gain confidence to apply for promotion as an international early career researcher. We then had an informal conversation over Zoom, where I was tossing an idea to her on writing on international academic experiences. She then said 'Why don't you take the lead?'. I still remember the conversation till today as I was caught by surprise – me as a junior researcher and that too an international academic who is trying to thrive in uncharted territory? I remember saying 'Me? You sure? I have not done this before'. Marian encouraged me and shared her wisdom with me on the process. I am forever grateful to her for this opportunity as I obtained knowledge on how the process works – to be an editor of a book (previously I was a chapter contributor only), fortunate to know other international scholars from around the world and rekindled with my colleagues, friends and acquittances to invite them to contribute to this book.

Actually, it was my dream to write on how international academics turn their issues into opportunities and adopt practical strategies that lead to successes within the Academy. Now that my dream is fulfilled, I do hope that this book will provide hope, inspiration and guidance to other aspiring international academics out there.

SETTING THE SCENE...

This book means a lot to me as an international academic myself, born and educated (up to undergraduate level) in Malaysia, I was intrigued to explore experiences of other international academics through a storytelling approach, with a practical lens. I completed my postgraduate degrees in Australia as an international student, and upon my PhD graduation I was employed on contract as an international academic in an Associate Lecturer position at my current institution.

Based on my experience, I noticed that international academics do not share with other colleagues (domestic or other international academics) about a number of things: (1) challenges they face or (2) opportunities they receive or even (3) strategies that they have adopted in their teaching and research endeavours as well as (4) celebrating their success or learning from their failures in the host higher learning institutions.

Hence, I wanted this book to offer an enhanced understanding of international academics' experiences, offering practical strategies and personal experiences, and using the BOSS (barriers, opportunities, strategies, successes) framework. I did not want to focus just on international academics' barriers and issues but most importantly I also wanted to highlight how they overturn their issues into opportunities and adopted successful strategies to gain varied success in the Academy. This framework is further explored in subsequent sections. I personally want to learn the trick and trades adopted by international academics globally, through a practical lens. This book is not based on theoretical or empirical research instead it is a sharing of the colourful journeys of international academics around the world through practical reflections. The chapters offer practical, hands-on individual stories of international academics that focus on the intersectionality of their experiences.

WHO ARE INTERNATIONAL ACADEMICS?

In the pursuit of internationalisation, progressively more higher education institutions are competing with one another to attract international academic staff members for a variety of reasons. Higher education institutions are keen to attract and host international academics, in order to propel their institutions in ranking systems, important for attracting international students and funding, as well as to fill gaps in staffing due to insufficient organic growth of research and teaching staff members (Burford, Koompraphant, & Jirathanapiwat, 2018; Gao & Liu, 2020; Larbi & Ashraf, 2020). Herschberg, Benschop, and van den Brink (2018) further argue that as a result of recruiting international academics, it 'will enhance quality related to research, education and service, which in turn, will lead to an enhanced international reputation' (p. 812) for the host institution. In addition, according to Kim, Wolf-Wendel, and Twombly (2011) international academics also 'bring with them a diversity of perspectives and worldviews that potentially enrich the university in the global context' (p. 722).

There are varied definitions of international academics. Scholars such as Kim et al. (2011) argue that prior research studies have skewedly defined international academics principally on their citizenship and birthplace excluding their immigration status, thus under-reporting the number of international academics. Therefore, Kim et al. (2011) define international academics as those who are foreign-born and gained undergraduate degrees in their home country as they 'may have very different cultural, social, and educational experiences that affect their academic life' (p. 723) while being employed in the host country higher learning institutions. Walker (2015) has another perspective of who international academics are. Walker (2015) argued that international academics are individuals who are born overseas, 'educated and enculturated in one system of education and currently teaching and researching in another' (Walker, 2015, p. 61). This definition is multidimensional as Walker (2015) does not specify if international academics gained their education either in their home or host or even third country.

For the purpose of this book, 'international academic' is defined as a foreign-born national employed at a host higher learning institution as a short-term or long-term teaching and/ or research staff member. Short-term mobility can be referred as visiting lecturer or researcher at the host higher learning institution for a short period of time (i.e. less than a year). For long-term mobility, an international academic is employed on teaching and research positions or research or teaching only positions for an extended period of time. In this instance, an international academic can also be a permanent residence or citizen of the host country.

CURRENT SCENE ON INTERNATIONAL ACADEMICS

As already noted, international academics bring 'a rich source of cultural, pedagogic and academic experience' (Minocha, Shiel, & Hristov, 2019, p. 943) to the host higher learning institutions due to their international backgrounds and vast experiences. The current literature on international academics demonstrates a number of unique strengths they offer to their host institutions. International academics leverage their international pedagogic practices, which can offer innovative solutions, such as introducing 'problem-based teaching and project-based learning, using rich media in the classroom and embedding international case studies' (Minocha et al., 2019, p. 952). In addition, international academics are often actively involved in the curriculum content development in their host institutions (Minocha et al., 2019). International academics have also contributed in the research space. For instance, international academics in Jepsen et al.'s (2014) study reported that they have established key international research collaborations and publications as well as being part of valuable research networks by working in an international setting. With achievements in teaching and research space, host higher education institutions have also benefitted from the cultural diversity of international academic staff members in enhancing quality of learning and research in universities (Green & Myatt, 2011).

Despite international academics' increasing presence and benefits they bring to host institutions, scholarly attention to international academics has been limited towards understanding international academics' personal and professional challenges, and it is usually reported as a one-dimensional or uniform experience (Sehoole, Adeyemo, Phatlane, & Ojo, 2019). Personal challenges include lack of communication with other colleagues due to language obstacles (Jiang et al., 2010; Wilkins & Neri, 2019), financial hardship due to relocation costs (Collins, 2008), adjustments to host-country ways of living and culture (Saltmarsh & Swirski, 2010; Wilkins & Neri, 2019), as well as issues with work permits (Wilkins & Neri, 2019).

Profound professional challenges include a lack of English proficiency for teaching students (Luxon & Peelo, 2009), differing approaches to teaching practices at their host institutions (Burford et al., 2018; Larbi & Ashraf, 2020; Singh & Chowdhury, 2021), different supervision practices (Jiang et al., 2010) and inadequate understanding of students' expectations and learning behaviours (Singh & Chowdhury, 2021).

Despite these challenges, international academics thrive in the Academy as they are highly educated and experienced individuals who have extraordinary competences, skills and abilities in academia but 'how' they have celebrated their success, overcome their personal and professional challenges as well as seized opportunities in different contexts is yet to be shared through their reflective experiences.

FUTURE SCENE USING BOSS FRAMEWORK...

Although empirical-based studies have provided valuable insights into the personal and professional challenges faced by international academics, they often neglect the ways in which international academics have adopted strategies and created opportunities in being competent teachers and researchers as well as benefitting other colleagues and students at their host university. Therefore, the BOSS framework is adopted in this book to explore the differing lenses and perspectives of international academics as early career researchers, leaders, mentors, LGBTIQ community advocates, family caregivers and short-term international academics. Their lived experiences are able to guide other international academics who are in similar situations or aspire to be an international academic in the future.

Key insights offered by the international academics in this book using the BOSS framework are as follows:

Ashleigh-Jane Thompson from New Zealand, currently a senior lecturer in one of the universities in Melbourne, Australia, wrote Chapter 1 highlighting her formal and informal leadership experiences as an early career international academic. How she obtained leadership positions in Australia as a woman in a male-dominated field is fascinating. You have to read the chapter to find out more!

Chapter 2 is written by Rui Hang, an Associate Vice President for Global Affairs at an American university. Through a philosophical lens, he explains how he transitioned from a 'plain' academic staff member from China to holding several senior leadership positions in the United States. You have to read his chapter on how he 'climbed' the leadership position and the professional and personal challenges that came with it.

A fascinating Chapter 3 by Vijay Kumar, from Malaysia and now attached to University of Otago, New Zealand (one of the most beautiful campuses in the world – I have been there myself – fantastic view) as an Associate Professor. He presents his insights on how he transitioned from being an academic in a Malaysian university to New Zealand. Vast difference, according to him. So, if you want to know more on his challenges, strategies he adopted and success stories, please do read his chapter.

Jinan Issa wrote her confronting experiences as an international scholar and a researcher in some of the MENA countries, Malaysia and Canada (Global North and South institutions) for over 14 years in Chapter 4. She has vast scholarly experience moving from country-to-country over 14 years. I would encourage you to read her chapter to gain more insight on how to be a mobile academic and highlights her recent move to Canada.

Chapter 5 offers a unique perspective from Muhammad Muftahu. Muhammad is from Nigeria and currently attached to a research institute in a Malaysian university. He mainly captures his experience as an international researcher by relating a few personal and professional issues that he encountered and proposes practical suggestions to overcome these challenges. If you are thinking of moving countries on an international researcher basis, I would read this chapter. Even for those seeking teaching and research positions, his experiences can be useful to advance your research career.

A profound international academic from India wrote about her international experiences working in Thailand, Malaysia and now currently based in China in Chapter 6. Amrita Kaur provides meaningful strategies on overcoming challenges as an international academic. If you want to know more about her academic opportunities as well as successes internationally, please do read her chapter.

It is tough to be an international academic more so an early career academic. So, in Chapter 7, Jasvir Kaur Nachatar Singh, from Malaysia, provides raw accounts on challenges she faced, how she created her own opportunities, adopted success strategies and how success came her way in Australia. Do not skip this chapter as you might find it useful to navigate your career path in academia using Jasvir's self-created opportunities.

Chapter 8 is written by Shannon Mason and Yusuke Sakurai from Japan. Shannon is from Australia and Yasuke is from Japan. An interesting account on how Shannon as an Australian navigates her career path in Japan and how

Yasuke, although from Japan, educated overseas is shocked with the academic system in Japan when he returned upon PhD graduation. I would not miss reading their chapter!

Another chapter from Japan but devised by husband and wife from Mongolia. Chapter 9 is composed by Ariunaa Enkhtur and Sainbayar Gundsambuu where they reflect on their journey as international academics with a young family. This will resonate with readers who are thinking of moving countries with a family. So don't skip this chapter as they provide useful advice for young families interested in working overseas especially in academia.

Chapter 10 is authored by Jisun Jung from Hong Kong where she relates her short-term mobility experiences in Australia. She describes her sabbatical experiences of a five-month international stay. So, if you are thinking of short-term mobility, do read this chapter as Jisun provides insights right from preparing to travel to returning home. So don't miss going through this chapter.

The final Chapter 11 is written by two academics who knew each other while working in a university in Thailand but both are from different parts of the world. If you want to know where they come from and how they bonded together as international academics, you have to read this chapter. They presented their experiences in a unique way – a conversational style approach – as well as from gender perspectives – you will be fascinated reading their chapter, for sure.

FINAL WORDS...

I do hope that this book will provide practical insights to aspiring international academics to excel in teaching and research endeavours at host institutions. In this book, the chapters are not only written by outstanding international academics with leadership positions or with excellent research and teaching outcomes but also by early career international academics, thereby offering an inspirational guide to current and future international academics. The flavour of this book is purposefully designed to cater to all academic levels around the globe. I sincerely wish that the readers will enjoy reading the varied chapters and resonate with them on personal and professional ground, as I have myself.

Send me an email (j.nachatarsingh@latrobe.edu.au or connect with me on LinkedIn) on your reflections and learnings from reading this book, and share with me the impact of this book on your personal and professional lives as an international academic. You might want to reflect after reading each chapter with these questions:

- What are your top three learning points?

- How do you relate these learning points to your experience?

- What steps would you like to take next in your career?

I would love to read your thoughts, and who knows we might create opportunities for future collaborations in this space!

REFERENCES

Burford, J., Koompraphant, G., & Jirathanapiwat, W. (2018). Being, adjusting and developing satisfaction: A review of ajarn tangchart (non-Thai academics) within the Thai higher education system. *Compare: A Journal of Comparative and International Education*, *50*(5), 656–675. doi:10.1080/03057925.2018.1544482

Collins, J. M. (2008). Coming to America: Challenges for faculty coming to United States' universities. *Journal of Geography in Higher Education*, *32*(2), 179–188. doi:10.1080/03098260701731215

Gao, Y., & Liu, J. (2020). Capitalising on academics' transnational experiences in the domestic research environment. *Journal of Higher Education Policy and Management*, *43*(4), 400–414. doi:10.1080/1360080X.2020.1833276

Green, W., & Myatt, P. (2011). Telling tales: A narrative research study of the experiences of new international academic staff at an Australian university. *International Journal for Academic Development*, *16*(1), 33–44. doi:10.1080/1360144X.2011.546219

Herschberg, C., Benschop, Y., & van den Brink, M. (2018). Selecting early-career researchers: The influence of discourses of internationalisation and excellence on formal and applied selection criteria in academia. *Higher Education*, *76*(5), 807–825.

Jepsen, D. M., Sun, J. J. M., Budhwar, P. S., Klehe, U. C., Krausert, A., Raghuram, S., & Valcour, M. (2014). International academic careers: Personal reflections. *The International Journal of Human Resource Management*, *25*(10), 1309–1326. doi:10.1080/09585192.2013.870307

Jiang, X., Di Napoli, R., Borg, M., Maunder, R., Fry, H., & Walsh, E. (2010). Becoming and being an academic: The perspectives of Chinese staff in two research-intensive UK universities. *Studies in Higher Education*, *35*(2), 155–170. doi:10.1080/03075070902995213

Kim, D., Wolf-Wendel, L., & Twombly, S. (2011). International faculty: Experiences of academic life and productivity in US universities. *The Journal of Higher*

Education, *82*(6), 720–747. doi:10.1080/00221546.2011.11777225

Larbi, F. O., & Ashraf, M. A. (2020). International academic mobility in Chinese academia: Opportunities and challenges. *International Migration*, *58*(3), 148–162. doi:10.1111/imig.12662

Luxon, T., & Peelo, M. (2009). Academic sojourners, teaching and internationalisation: The experience of non-UK staff in a British University. *Teaching in Higher Education*, *14*(6), 649–659. doi:10.1080/13562510903315233

Minocha, S., Shiel, C., & Hristov, D. (2019). International academic staff in UK higher education: Campus internationalisation and innovation in academic practice. *Journal of Further and Higher Education*, *43*(7), 942–958. doi:10.1080/0309877X.2018.1429582

Saltmarsh, S., & Swirski, T. (2010). 'Pawns and prawns': International academics' observations on their transition to working in an Australian university. *Journal of Higher Education Policy and Management*, *32*(3), 291–301. doi:10.1080/13600801003743505

Sehoole, C., Adeyemo, K. S., Phatlane, R., & Ojo, E. (2019). Academic mobility and the experiences of foreign staff at South African higher education institutions. *South African Journal of Higher Education*, *33*(2), 212–229.

Singh, J. K. N., & Chowdhury, H. (2021). Early-career international academics' learning and teaching experiences during COVID-19 in Australia: A collaborative autoethnography. *Journal of University Teaching and Learning Practice*, *18*(5), 1–17.

Walker, P. (2015). The globalisation of higher education and the sojourner academic: Insights into challenges experienced by newly appointed international academic staff in a UK university. *Journal of Research in International Education*, *14*(1), 61–74.

Wilkins, S., & Neri, S. (2019). Managing faculty in transnational higher education: Expatriate academics at international branch campuses. *Journal of Studies in International Education*, *23*(4), 451–472. doi:10.1177/1028315318814200

Section 1

LEADERSHIP

1

BREAKING THROUGH THE GLASS CEILING: NAVIGATING TOWARDS LEADERSHIP POSITIONS AS A WOMAN INTERNATIONAL ACADEMIC

Ashleigh-Jane Thompson

ABSTRACT

While emerging research suggests that women have made great gains within the higher education sector, significant challenges remain. Notably, women are still severely under-represented in leadership positions in the academe, and this is even more so for international academics. As an early-career academic, I am fortunate that my journey so far has allowed me to hold various leadership positions (both informal and formal). In this book chapter, I reflect on my own experiences. In so doing, I share insights into how to be an 'opportunist' in gaining leadership positions as a woman, breaking through the glass ceiling – that symbolic obstacle women hit – while being an international academic. The chapter starts with a brief overview of my background and my non-traditional pathway into

the Sport Management discipline more broadly and the
sub-discipline where I now feel at 'home'. In what follows,
I consider how some of the barriers and challenges I faced
along the way have served to shape my future self. It is,
perhaps, not without some degree of irony, that strategies
I developed to mitigate or overcome these led to what I
term self-created opportunities. The chapter then reflects
on some of the successes I have achieved.

Keywords: Leadership; international early career
academic; challenges; opportunities; strategies; successes

WHERE IT ALL STARTED

To contextualise the reflections and experiences that I draw
from in the following sections, it is important to provide an
introduction and overview of who I am and what has shaped
my resulting international academic identity. I was born in
New Zealand (NZ) where I grew up and completed all my
education. Like many fellow 'Kiwis', my ancestry provides
strong ties to the United Kingdom (UK) and Ireland, where
dreams of undertaking an overseas experience (OE) abound.
My maternal grandmother immigrated to New Zealand as a
young adult but her continued passion and love for all things
'British', along with visits from extended relatives from
Ireland and the United Kingdom, sparked my curiosity about
the world beyond New Zealand's shores. Not surprisingly, I
was a passionate student of social science at school, most
notably drawn to history, sociology, cultural studies and
languages (Japanese and French). All of these experiences

planted and cultivated my desire to, at some point, discover life abroad.

However, I also developed other interests in technology and computing which led me to complete a Bachelor's degree in Computer Science. I was fortunate enough to be awarded a postgraduate scholarship to continue for an Honours year. Till this point, I had been privileged. This was the first time I found myself in the position of being part of a minority group. During this period, women in Science, Technology, Engineering and Maths (STEM) disciplines were few and far between as it was, and perhaps still is, a very male-dominated area. In my final year, I was often the sole woman in my classes, and soon, the notion of being different or the 'odd one out' became the norm. Throughout my studies, I became socialised into the norms of what it meant to exist, within this male-dominated space. While I was fortunate to have peers, lecturers and supervisors who treated me with respect and embraced my presence this was not always the case. I recall a conversation not long after I received my first job offer as a developer for a leading IT company that left me taken aback. The crux of it was that, in their view, I was fortunate – I ticked an inclusion box that would give me an automatic advantage over others. For them, the fact I was a woman far outweighed my skills and ability which they saw as secondary (I received a scholarship as one of the top 5% of undergraduates completing a degree across the entire College of Sciences – so I guess I did know something). Unfortunately, it is a sentiment that I have encountered several times since.

I declined that job offer and instead took time off to travel overseas. It was here, in the United Kingdom while watching a game of tennis, my career path changed. Swapping one male-dominated industry for another, I embarked on a journey into the Sport Management field. Fast forward several years, and after completing a Postgraduate Diploma in Business Administration and a PhD at Massey University (New Zealand) I entered the world of academia full-time in 2016. While worked as a casual tutor and lecturer throughout my studies, I received a fixed-term contract as a Lecturer at Massey University just before submitting my PhD. As anyone who has been in a contract position knows, the uncertainty of future employment is not always easy, and so I began looking for other opportunities. With a limited number of positions in my discipline in New Zealand, I saw gaining employment at an international institution as a beneficial career move. Fortunately, in 2017, I was offered a full-time, continuing Lecturer's position with the Department of Management, Sport and Tourism at La Trobe University, Australia.

As the following sections will show, I consider myself to be an international academic across two dimensions. Firstly, in the more literal sense, I was born, educated and started my academic career overseas. Secondly, in the teaching, research and service domains, I have worked to develop extensive networks with colleagues and peers overseas that has created an element of 'internationality' to my work. I think it is also important, at this point, to acknowledge that leadership can, and often does, take many different forms. As Donald McGannon, an American broadcasting industry executive and devoted advocate for social responsibility in the media, once said 'leadership is an action, not a position'. Indeed, leadership is not simply about the role or title one holds within an organisation or the academy more broadly. Rather, it is the action we choose to take, the choices and the behaviours. It is with this lens, and these considerations, that I share insights on the barriers, opportunities, strategies and successes that I have experienced to date. While some are specific to my journey, I hope that others may see value in these, as they seek to break through the glass ceiling.

THE LEADERSHIP LABYRINTH: BARRIERS ALONG THE WAY

Research is replete with literature documenting certain barriers and obstacles that women and international academics face in ascending to leadership positions in higher education (see Helms, Schendel, Godwin, & Blanco, 2021). So here, I will instead focus on my own personal lived experiences. While I have not had to contend with significant cultural differences or language barriers in my international academic journey, one of the biggest challenges has been navigating the subtle nuances of new work cultures and different institutional expectations while still striving to deliver the best possible learning experience for students. That said, I do feel like there is a sense that certain cultural values do shape this experience. For example, in Australia I have found that it is not feminine to aspire to, or identify as, a leader, while in New Zealand there exists a certain tall-poppy syndrome, where you do not overtly promote yourself as a leader. Coming to a new international institution there was also this sense of trying to work out and identify the who's who of the institutional network. Who are the people that need to know who you are if you aspire to be in a formal position of leadership? The ability to build your profile and network becomes extremely important, something I expand on in the following section.

Being based on a regional (outskirts of Melbourne) campus presented challenges in the acculturation process as I tried to understand the subtle and nuanced differences between New Zealand and Australian higher education systems. I was also the sole staff member in my discipline which created a literal geographic and figurative barrier to creating meaningful connections with colleagues within my discipline and the department, often sparked by those informal 'water-cooler' conversations. In some respects, I was, by default, the lone wolf who adapted to the environment by taking ownership of a small piece of something I could meaningfully contribute to becoming the Course Advisor for our regional degrees. This proved to be the stepping stone to my next formal leadership position when a year after joining the University, I took on a formal leadership position as the Program Director for the Sport Management suite of courses.

While I did not set out initially with a clear short- or long-term career plan that included any formal leadership positions, I had the lofty ambition of one day being considered a leader, whether it be in research or teaching. As research shows, I knew this would be a challenging process. When I considered the experiences of colleagues who I looked up to and aspired to be like, I saw that leadership opportunities for women and international academics were hard enough to attain at the culmination of a long career, let alone for an early career academic starting their journey. It felt like to be successful there was a game to be played, a system to be unlocked or a secret code to be cracked, and this was something that never resonated with me.

Another barrier that I am still trying to overcome is the persistent struggle with feelings of self-doubt that has materialised more within the context of formal leadership positions I hold or have held. As I noted earlier, there have been times throughout my career when I felt others had assumed, albeit wrongly, that I got a position solely because I ticked a box – I was a woman, I was based at a certain location, I was young. That said, there have also been situations where my youth has been perceived as a disadvantage when age has been used as a proxy for experience. This has often made me feel insecure and caused me to question and doubt my abilities. This is not a point that I have shared openly with many others before, and I know I am not alone in this. This notion of the imposter syndrome is something that is also a sentiment shared by others.

Finally, although I have never publicly voiced this before, one of the things I struggled with as an early-career researcher (ECR), and to some extent still do, was trying to work out just where I fit. I looked to leaders who excelled in teaching, who had stellar research reputations and others who contributed heavily in academic citizenship. I tried to find the magic formula that would allow me to do it all, be involved in all aspects of an academic's role, but one was not apparent. If I focused on research, I had less time for service-related activities. If I took on more service activities I had less time to devote to innovative teaching. I have been fortunate to encounter an amazing mentor who keeps telling me, there's not a 'right way' to do things, just 'your way', if being a well-rounded academic is what fulfils you keep at it.

SPOTLIGHTING OPPORTUNITIES AND STRATEGIES

Without trying to be overly simplistic, for me, some of the key strategies that have contributed to various informal and formal leadership positions or roles I have been involved with are (1) taking advantage of opportune moments, (2) leveraging my internationalism, (3) building a profile and developing networks and (4) finding good mentors.

I have learnt that it is important for those in formal leadership positions to have institutional credibility and knowledge. Additionally, depending on the leadership role, knowledge and understanding of the broad higher education sector and national and international trends is advantageous. I am fortunate that I took advantage of serendipitous opportunities that enabled me to develop these insights earlier on. For example, during my postgraduate studies, I undertook casual work as an administrator in our Campus Registrar's Office. Here, I was exposed to participation in the Campus Life committee, Sports Forum and Academic Leadership Forum. I also worked on various initiatives and strategies designed to support and enhance student progression and distance student education. At the time, the drawcard was a monetary benefit. However, in hindsight, that experience has been invaluable in allowing me to develop the big picture understanding and global view that has enhanced my strategic thinking.

Additionally, one of the foremost barriers that many women face in the academy more broadly is the realities of careering and familial responsibilities that often dispropor-tionally fall to them. In my case, it was not the presence of these obligations that presented a challenge, but rather the lack of them. When I started my academic career, I was one of only a few staff members in my school who were deemed to be free of such obligations. This led to requests to attend func-tions, events, or other activities because I was 'free'. In hind-sight, my innate inability to say no to things, something I continue to struggle with, meant that I participated in activ-ities that allowed me to build networks and a profile within contexts that I would not have been exposed to otherwise. Now, here I am not advocating that others follow my path and, in a do as I say not as I do moment, saying no is an important skill to develop. However, the lesson in this is being open to opportunities that present themselves. Particularly if it provides you with the ability to expand your network and put you in front of people who you consider to be influential in your field, discipline, or institution. Just be selective with those that you say yes to!

One thing that I have come to realise over time is that there is a distinction to be made between being 'an' international academic and being 'the' international academic. In this sense,

I mean considering your internationalism as a benefit that can be leveraged by way of the insights, experiences and knowledge of 'other' contexts that you can contribute to teaching, research and academic citizenship as not only a leader but an academic citizen more broadly. For example, I recognised that there was, to some extent, an over-abundance of research and researchers in my specific research area from the Global North, particularly in North America and Canada. I saw this as an opportunity for me to position myself as an emerging leader within the field that could offer a unique understanding of the context within the Global South. I acknowledge upfront the privileged position that afforded me with the following opportunities to achieve this and recognise that for others this may not be possible. Initially, international conference attendance was one of the key mechanisms through which I sought to leverage my international-ness. While COVID-19 has created challenges with international travel, the benefit has been the enhanced global accessibility of conferences and events with opportunities for virtual attendance.

As someone who would not self-identify as being overly extroverted, the idea of putting myself out there to build a profile and develop networks was a challenging proposition. While I had colleagues who could self-promote like rock stars, this was something I initially felt uncomfortable at the thought of doing. However, I quickly learnt that I needed to move from being *out of sight* to *being visible* with other leaders. So, I focused on doing so in a way that showcased the impact or contribution that I felt I was making. Another tactic that I have used to build my profile and allow me to demonstrate leadership within both formal and non-formal dimensions is the translation of my work within the local community. Something I considered important as someone new here. While based in Bendigo this has been achieved through my active role as a Board member on three sports organisations' boards: Proud2Play, Bendigo Tennis Association (BTA) and the Bendigo Academy of Sport. More recently, as I have gained confidence, I have also sought to engage with the media (i.e. print, radio and television) as an outlet to translate my research, encourage public dialogue and debate and raise my profile.

In terms of networking, I leveraged opportunities and situations that would allow the ability to connect with others in a safe and supportive environment. These can be either internal or external to your institution. For example, I used social media to make connections with scholars and educators whose work resonated or influenced me. When we met in person, we had already established a rapport. I initially attended conferences and events that were deemed to be the best in our discipline but often felt out of place. When I shifted my focus to ones that complemented my specific interest area, I felt like I had found my people, and the networking became easier as we connected over our shared common interest. A simple chat with a colleague over a mutual interest in tennis following a presentation led to a collaboration on an international research funding proposal and invitations to visit their institution as a visiting scholar.

I also looked for opportunities to get involved in other formal or informal networks that supported women and international colleagues. An informal group that has helped me acclimate to the Australian system and that supports women in the male-dominated sport discipline is the cheekily named Brainy Sport Ladies group. I consider several members of this group to also be important career mentors. For me, finding great mentors has been one of the most important things I have done. To find these elusive mentors, I have joined institutional mentorship programmes, discipline association mentorship initiatives, and more recently, reached out to colleagues and role models directly seeking mentorship in specific areas. I have also provided mentorship to colleagues in social media data collection and analysis methods and supported their publishing endeavours via formal and informal discussions and peer review activities.

CELEBRATE SUCCESS: BUT WHAT DOES IT LOOK LIKE?

As I reflect on some of the things I would consider some of my successes to date, another barrier to be acknowledged at this point is the lack of uniformity in defining what success is. Taking the time to reflect on these points, to pause and recognise these as things worth celebrating has been a bit of a cathartic process. I encourage others to also take a break from the 'busy-ness' of work-life and celebrate your success no matter how big or small. Each one is contributing to your journey, building your profile and developing your leadership potential.

Within the teaching domain, in my role as Program Director, I have endeavoured to share my passion for providing a positive contribution to subject and curriculum development and ensuring the innovative subject design and delivery. Students often appreciate my engaging and approachable teaching style that challenges their ways of thinking, and this is reflected in the consistently high scores I have received in student feedback surveys. My work has also been recognised nationally and internationally within my discipline. I have been invited to create professional development courses for industry, guest lecture to students in undergraduate classes from two North American institutions and have presented a webinar on online teaching to 40 participants worldwide. I have also organised and moderated two webinars on scholarly teaching in Sport Management. I am also the first, and to date only, academic at my institution to have published a teaching case study, with international colleagues, in *Case Studies in Sport Management*, the only journal dedicated to case studies in the discipline. One of the things I am most proud of is not a personal success, but the success of my students who have gone on to thrive post-study and who have secured full-time positions in academia in the current tumultuous tertiary sector.

Within the research space, I have received invites to share my research nationally and internationally. In 2017, I was invited by the Royal Society of New Zealand to give a public lecture as part of their Sharing Women's Discoveries' 150th Anniversary celebrations, and in 2019 I provided a public lecture at the University of Washington State. In 2019, I also received an Emerald Literati Outstanding Paper Award from the *Sport, Business and Management*. Sport Australia's Clearinghouse for Sport knowledge base, Canada's Sport Information Research Centre (SIRC) and the Polish Triathlon knowledge base have all featured my research. The research included on these platforms is used to inform policy and practice within the broader Australian and international sport context. Additionally, findings from my research were used to inform recommendations on mapping future competencies for sport managers presented in an Erasmus + report. A highlight that links to the internationalisation that is a feature of my career to date has been the collaborative research networks, with respected international scholars, that I have been able to foster and grow. Notably, over half of my research outputs in the past five years have been with international collaborators (e.g. from the United States, United Kingdom and Canada).

It is within the academic citizenship or service space where I have had more formal leadership roles. Within my role as Program Director for Sport Management, I have established the disciplines first Course Advisory Committee, led a major curriculum review, developed an online community of practice and have overseen the development and delivery of a new diploma course with one of our sporting partners. Alongside this, I have been a passionate advocate for advancing research and the scholarship of teaching and learning within the discipline by leading, or contributing to, several new initiatives. This has been achieved largely over the past five years during my time on the Sport Management of Australia and New Zealand's (SMAANZ) Board, where I was recently elected as Vice-President for 2021–2022. My small successes in leadership within the discipline also include Editorial Board membership and regular ad-hoc review activities for leading journals and publishers.

IT IS NOT A SPRINT…

In writing this chapter, and reflecting on my journey, I have asked myself if there is a piece of advice, I wish my future self could have imparted. For the most part, despite some of the struggles and challenges along the way, there is not much I would change. Perhaps though, the one thing that comes to mind is the rush with which I sought to tick off all those things that that influential leaders in academia have done. In doing so, assuming leadership positions so early in my career meant that this was often at the expense of participating in other ECR experiences or opportunities. Leaning into my Sport Management roots here – it's not a sprint. Perhaps it is not even a race.

I am far from the finish line. My journey continues, and I look forward to seeing where it takes me next. I hope that sharing my story might resonate with others. Inspiring and encouraging others as they navigate their career. Being a woman and an international academic can be challenging, particularly when it comes to being in a leadership role. I am fortunate to currently work at an institution that is committed to achieving equality in its operations. Transformative change is required across the sector to ensure more international women achieve and sustain leadership positions. To achieve this, we can contribute to change by supporting and recognising 'women leaders as intentional, strategic, intelligent, deliberate, goal-driven, focused, accomplished, successful, ambitious and visionary' (Alcalde & Subramaniam, 2020).

REFERENCES

Alcalde, M. C., & Subramaniam, M. (2020, July 17). Women in leadership: Challenges and recommendations. *Inside Higher Ed*. Retrieved from https://www.insidehighered.com/views/2020/07/17/women-leadership-academe-still-face-challenges-structures-systems-and-mind-sets

Helms, R. M., Schendel, R., Godwin, K., & Blanco, G. (2021). Women's representation in higher education leadership around the world. *International Briefs for Higher Education Leaders*, 9. Retrieved from https://www.acenet.edu/Documents/Womens-Rep-in-Higher-Ed-Leadership-Around-the-World.pdf

2

VIRTUOUS LIKE WATER – INTERNATIONAL ACADEMIC IN A LEADERSHIP POSITION

Yuhang Rong

ABSTRACT

This chapter presents personal lessons that I have learned as an international academic from China to the United States, through my journey from an academic staff member to senior leadership positions in the field of education. Through overcoming barriers and seeking opportunities, I have learned the strategies of knowing ourselves, thinking critically, willingness to work on thankless assignments, broadening horizons, traveling, and ultimately, enjoying what we do.

Keywords: International academic; international career; higher education; China; United States; career development

上善若水。水善利万物而不争, 处众人之所恶, 故几
于道。

-老子《道德经》第八章

The highest human virtue is to be like water, which is good at nourishing everything but does not compete with it. It always stays in low-lying places where people don't want to go. This kind of character is the closest to 'Tao'.

–Laozi (approximately 516 B.C.) *Tao Te Ching*,
Chapter 8

Raised and educated in China, I learned how one's life, a nation's economy and security could be impacted by the political and natural environment of the world. To understand the intricacies and complications of people's interactions, I realized that academics must possess global perspectives and know what their colleagues are achieving around the world. Being an academic, one must be willing and able to cross international borders in action and in thoughts. An international academic could benefit by functioning like water.

In America, most believe the academic career path is a one-way street. After earning a terminal degree, an academic must secure a tenure-track faculty position at a university, and teach and publish papers in order to reach full professorship. Once there, they may venture into leadership roles, such as department heads, deans, provosts, eventually presidents.

The challenge for someone like me to hold senior academic leadership positions at a top research university is almost impossible because I never traveled down this one-way street. Through luck and hard work, however, I have succeeded to an extent. My teachers and mentors taught me to constantly assess my knowledge and skills to ensure they are compatible with the task at hand. They taught me logical and critical thinking skills for problem-solving. They taught me to be humble and to be willing to do thankless jobs at which I excel. Most importantly, they taught me to seek creative solutions by connecting knowledge and people. The addition of travel has fostered professional collaborations. I learned how to grasp opportunities when they arise and to employ strategies to keep them. Ultimately, I learned to behave like water – focusing on what is in my pathway and being flexible while carrying on toward the right destination.

KNOW YOURSELF

One of my mentors said: 'Do what you are good at. If you want to do something you are not good at, then get good at it fast'. Knowing what you are good at requires self-assessment and reflection. Chick (2013) defines this critical aspect of learning and development, often referred to as metacognition, as 'the processes used to plan, monitor and assess one's understanding and performance'.

A strong academic is one who can capitalise on what he is good at, comfortable with and loves. This may sound easy, but it requires skills of constant evaluation and recalibration to reach career goals. Many of the jobs I chose were very challenging. Before committing, I usually conduct an honest mental self-assessment of my knowledge and skills to determine whether I could be successful in the particular organisational environment. I did not seek positions based on whether they are a right step on a conventional career ladder. My approach afforded me a sense of freedom that I may not otherwise have enjoyed.

The mental self-assessments have taught me to be aware of my personal dispositions. Am I content to be a small fish in a big pond, or would I want to be a big fish in a small pond? Some may even want to be a big fish in a big pond. All of these choices represent significant trade-offs in determining factors of personal ego, financial compensation, organisational culture and types of colleagues the position interacts. For me, while institutional reputation is an important factor when I choose positions, I personally value the working environment much more – will I have a supportive and trustworthy team? Is this an organisation that needs the best of my knowledge and skills?

My family and teachers fostered these skills in me from an early age. As a child, my criteria for a career was based solely on a fun factor. In kindergarten, I wanted to be a driver for Shanghai's No. 20 bus. This bus traveled between the east and west sides of the city center and stopped at all the great places: the Bund, the Nanjing Road shopping district, the Park Hotel (at the time, the tallest building in the city), art deco movie theatres, a Buddhist temple and parks and wide avenues shaded by rows of plane trees. In elementary school, I dreamed of being a movie projectionist, like Toto in Giuseppe Tornatore's nostalgic *Cinema Paradiso*. To me, it was the ideal job. I could watch all the newly released films – for free!

I made my most unconventional and most consequential career choice in high school. I came from a family of engineers. I was expected to become an engineer, or at least a medical doctor or a scientist.

In the early 1980s, there were only enough spaces in China's universities for about 5% of high school graduates. Competition was fierce. The single most important measure was a high score on the college entrance examination, known as *gaokao*. The last two years of high school instruction focused on preparation for the *gaokao*. For the first time in my schooling, I felt an incredible amount of pressure and started to have a sensation of drowning in subjects like chemistry.

Taking *gaokao* in the science track was not fun for me. I felt I did not have the mental tenacity and skills that would get me into a top university.

I did have a talent for and a love of the English language. It was definitely fun to be able to communicate with people who spoke no Chinese and to read great stories such as *The Old Man and the Sea*. It gave me a sense of life in other parts of the world. I began to imagine not only passing the *gaokao* in the humanity track but also achieving a high score. I wanted to get into a great college and excel in humanities.

So, at the dinner table one warm spring evening during my junior year in high school, I dropped the bomb: 'I don't want to take my college entrance exam in the science track. I will take the humanity track'.

Their reaction reminded me of film footage of a nuclear explosion: momentary silence followed by a flash. My grandparents, my mother and my two engineer uncles, froze, mid-chew and stared at me.

Then began a barrage of cries and questions like 'how could you?' 'how dare you!' to 'what will you study?' and 'how will you make a living?'

It was my grandmother – the only one at the dinner table who did not have a college degree – who finally quieted the others: 'The child should be able to make his own choice as long as he is willing to deal with the consequences'. 40 years later, I can honestly say I have never regretted that decision and I am forever grateful to my grandmother for her support. That was the first successful outcome after month-long mental self-assessment of my own capacity.

THINK CRITICALLY LIKE A MATHEMATICIAN

Although I happily abandoned my family's wishes, I recognise that mathematics and science taught me logical and critical thinking skills that have served me well as an international academic. One of my college professors later told me that even though my total *gaokao* scores were not the highest, they were impressed that I took the optional mathematics examination and scored 95%. He explained that anyone who can earn a high score on a mathematics examination can achieve anything in life because they can think critically. Mathematics helped me to creatively solve problems because I learned that there are many ways to address an issue. Some solutions take longer and some cost more money but the ability to think outside the box is a useful skill that achieves results. Mathematics taught me to think like a chess player, to think ahead and to know the players involved.

Mathematics helped me in my language learning and in my writing. I would lay out my arguments, data and other supporting evidence like a mathematics problem, placing all factors for consideration on either side of the equation.

'What is the issue?' 'What is the research question?' These questions are from two of my greatest teachers, who profoundly influenced how I make decisions and solve problems. I took two educational law courses in my graduate studies. My law professor assigned us to read legal briefs before each class. During class, she would ask this simple question for each case: 'What is the issue?' She helped us to extract all the non-essential facts surrounding the legal argument to ensure that we identified the key question. After weeks of this exercise, I learned how to identify critical issues and to not let side stories blur the lines.

My doctoral program advisor consistently asked, 'What is the research question?' As a research methodologist, he taught us to avoid the common mistake of developing research methods before solidifying the research question. This placing-cart-in-front-of-horse method has contributed to low quality dissertations and prolonged the time to degree completion.

Like mathematics, these ideas have served as guiding principles in my problem-solving process. Many people in the academe throw everything but the kitchen sink into problem solving. The ability to isolate issues and focus on the root cause of problems have helped me to succeed. In academic leadership roles, these are critically important skills.

LOSE YOUR EGO

The academe is notorious for its egos. This is especially true at top-ranked research institutions. Yet, not all have fallen into the trap of egoism. There are many successful researchers who have not only published prominent research findings but also have had their research applied in everyday products. Many of these people are down-to-earth, modest individuals. Yet egos exist and persist in higher education. One of my colleagues once remarked that the more mediocre the person, the greater the ego.

Cellist Yo-Yo Ma (2021) advises musicians to consider the needs of their audience and the value they can bring to the lives of their listeners. In essence, when they perform Bach or Beethoven, the goal is not to showcase their techniques, it is to move their audience. He said, 'When you perform, it's the person you're playing for that is the most important in the room, and that's not you... If you are there to share something important, [the audience] have to get it and it has to live in them for it to be meaningful and purposeful'.

This logic may be applied to academics. The point is not to promote their own knowledge, it is to demonstrate success as measured by outcome: the outcome of student learning; the results of their research; and the quality of their services to their academic community.

A previous assignment required me to ensure that the university met national accreditation standards. A professor commented on my predicament: 'You have a thankless job. If it went well, faculty will garner all the credit; if it goes badly, you get the blame'.

I considered this when preparing my initial remarks to the faculty. How can I help the faculty to understand that accreditation review is really about their successes. I used the analogy of coordinating an accreditation review is like wrapping a gift. The faculty creates the gift, I make sure the gift is in a beautiful box, wrapped in designer paper, topped with a gorgeous bow. But no matter how pretty the gift looks, the accreditation review team needs to see and play with the gift. In the end, the product matters. The real academic work belonged to the faculty; I would serve as the 'clean up' person. We worked together as a great team and the outcomes were two cycles of enormously successful national accreditation reviews.

A senior university leader jokingly told me the secret of my relatively successful career: 'Everyone likes you because you have no ambition'. He intended it as a compliment, meaning I had never plotted or conspired to get the next position or higher pay. Instead, I worked with everyone on campus to get the job done, striving always to be effective without being threatening. As a result, when positions opened up, people would often think of me. In this respect, perhaps, I am ambitious; I just achieve my goals in unconventional ways.

BROADEN THE HORIZON

The phrase 'He's a jack of all trades, master of none' no longer applies to today's world. Today's international academics must learn to become a 'jack of all trades'.

Over the last 30 years, the world has witnessed ground-breaking and lightning speed developments in science and technology. Rifkin (2011) observes human relations are shifting from hierarchical to lateral, and that the world's economies are no longer defined by siloed industrious fields. Rapid progress in information technology carries the risk of unintended consequences posing the greatest challenge to democracy. It has never been more essential for academics to foster in-depth knowledge and skills across disciplines; to engage in critical thinking; to be creative; to collaborate and communicate; and to utilize information, media and technology to our advantage. We must work collaboratively across disciplines to solve problems. Being a 'jack of all trades' may be more important in today's world than ever before.

When I was young, one of my uncles made me draw pictures (in addition to my grandmother's calligraphy assignments). I grudgingly complied but eventually I found these activities relaxing especially because I could listen to music or film soundtracks at the same time. These exercises cultivated in me an appreciation for art and music which complemented my academic learning, lending unique perspectives on problem solving. The concept of negative space – blank spaces in paintings that form an integral part of the entire composition – taught me the importance of inaction in the problem-solving process. One of my mentors taught me to listen carefully when a problem is presented. With careful questioning, the solution could be self-evident to the presenter of the problem. Rather than always rushing to solve a problem, sometimes, the best solution is to do nothing. Knowing when to act (or not) requires skill and an ability to recognise that some of problems are more transient, that time would have solved them.

Today's academics must work with colleagues across disciplines and be willing to move around. While I have not worked outside of the State of Connecticut in the last 30 years, I have changed jobs in the interval of four to eight years, from student affairs, academic regulations and international collaborations in both universities and governmental agencies. I have served on the boards of non-profit organisations and national accreditation agencies. I have had the good fortune to work with colleagues from all over the world and have visited and collaborated with their teams in their home countries. Once, after successfully completing a consulting project in a middle east university, the colleagues said, 'Now you are one of us'. *That* – unification – is the ultimate goal of education: the ability to recognise that there is only 'us' there is no 'them'.

A prominent philanthropist reflected the notion that many people thought he was very lucky to have had wonderful business opportunities. He recognised the lucks he had. However, he emphasised that when lucks knocked on his door, he was ready for them.

I have tried to follow his advice. The traditional academic prepares to work in a specialty field by traveling down that one-way street. The further along he gets, the more the path narrows. This is the nature of becoming a specialist in a chosen field. Our systems encourage and reward depth but not necessarily breath. I often joke with colleagues that I have a mild case of 'attention deficit hyperactivity disorder'. But the reality is that I always wanted to be ready for opportunities that might fall beyond my chosen field of study. I don't like to be 'bored' at doing the same things again and again. I like new challenges requiring a wider variety of experiences.

SEE THE WORLD

Intercultural competences are essential to successful international academics. Pinto (2018) explains that

> ...[a]cademics recognize the multidimensionality of intercultural competence, acknowledging that it comprises attitudes (acceptance and respect; curiosity and openness), knowledge (others' cultural contexts; self-knowledge and cultural self-awareness) and skills (observation and listening) that altogether will lead to individuals' desired internal and external outcomes. The development of intercultural competence... is considered crucial for changing prejudiced attitudes, preparing students to live in a global world and empowering them professionally.

In college, I was not a straight A student though overall I performed well. What was equally important in the long run was the fact that my professors mentored me for student leadership opportunities and encouraged me to read and participate in cultural events the city had to offer. I ventured out of my normal curricular activities to seek other experiences, including reading outdated issues of *The New York Times* and, occasionally, *Newsweek* and *Time* magazines, and taking part time jobs doing simultaneous translation of foreign films. My first publication was a short blurb introducing Chinua Achebe's *Things Fall Apart* to a Chinese audience. I was the first in China to translate Ernest Hemingway's article on Spanish Civil War. I taught Chinese to foreign students and traveled with them around China. From them I learned about frivolous, but uniquely cultural things like TV sitcoms and fashion brands. All these experiences made my transition as an international student in American universities much smoother. I not only knew the technical aspects of the English language, I also learned how it applied in situations and real-world circumstances. I had less issues of comprehension and participation in courses and seminars, and more importantly, making friends.

Poet Su Shi (1084) observed that 'one can't see the shape of the mountain when one lives on the mountain'. For an international academic, this means that they must branch out to more related fields and disciplines. Being confined to a narrow topic, in general, will not foster new knowledge and innovative ideas. Science, art, music and mathematics are interconnected and the academic who is well-versed in multiple disciplines has a higher chance of not only being successful, but of contributing to a global society where there is only 'us' and no 'them'. In my role as the senior leader representing the university in a global research university consortium, I have had the privilege of visiting many universities around the world. Each time, I would inevitably compare models of operation and learn a great deal of these universities. I have gained better perspectives of the strengths and areas for improvement for my own university.

The essence of my experiences and of this chapter can be reduced to one concept: travel. Nothing resonates more with me than the following quotation from the late Anthony Bourdain (2006): 'Travel changes you. As you move through this life and this world you change things slightly, you leave marks behind, however small. And in return, life – and travel – leaves marks on you'. Contemporary academics must literally and figuratively travel, but also learn and apply knowledge across disciplines. Rapid discoveries and development of knowledge can only happen when we cross borders and boundaries.

LOSE YOUR CAREER PLAN AND ENJOY THE RIDE

It is always a good idea to map out the general direction of one's professional career steps. While one learns knowledge and skills for their chosen profession, they should keep in mind how to apply what they have learned to other fields. For a long time since my graduate school days, I religiously pursued all the steps for a career in higher education student affairs. I made sure that I developed a network with mentors and colleagues in the field through my participation in conferences, keeping myself updated on new research and best practices, joining key organisations like the American College Personnel Association and becoming members to various standing committees, and seeking recognitions whenever appropriate. I almost had a mental checklist and made sure I checked off all the items on the list.

The most significant professional opportunity came to me through the connection of my doctoral advisor. I was invited to apply for a federal grant administrator position by the office of the state commissioner of education. The position was to manage two grants up to $2 million for K-12 school teacher recruitment, especially those who were in shortage subject areas and from diverse backgrounds. I was surprised. I had no experience working in K-12 education. But I was encouraged to seek this opportunity because of my project management skills, and knowledge in research design. I was also told that it seemed to them that I knew how to work with people.

From this position, I worked with colleagues not only in my home state but also with colleagues across the country. It built a solid foundation for my later work in higher education program approval, accreditation, budget allocation and management, and international collaboration. I learned how to work with diverse and sometimes political constituencies and build consensus. My subsequent positions as an assistant dean and associate vice president all happened naturally through various transition among organisations as people start to recognize my capacities.

It was good that I had a general career plan with some key goals and objectives. I, however, learned that we should also let it go as career transitions may take place naturally because of one's accomplishments and abilities. This is a luxury that traditional academics who travel down the narrow one-way street may never be able to afford. Sometimes, it is simply great to enjoy the ride.

CONCLUSION

My professional experience does not need to be exceptional. An academic career does not have to be a narrow one-way street. There are many opportunities and functions in universities that await talented and dedicated individuals. In Hawai'i, there is a value described as 'nānā i ke kumu' which means 'look to your source'. It is about seeking authenticity, being true to ourselves, as well as honoring and remembering those who went before us. Say (2016) explains that it means to become more self-aware.

Successful academics learn to be self-aware through constant self-assessment. They do not speak unless they have something useful to say. They do not force themselves onto others but rather they let their accomplishments speak. They flow through their environment like water. They bring nourishment and solutions to their work place, yet they do not threaten their colleagues or institutions. When they encounter obstacles, they find alternate paths to continue their journey. If they flow like water, all their goals in teaching, learning, research and service can be achieved.

REFERENCES

Bourdain, A. (2006). *The nasty bits: Collected varietal cuts, useable trim, scraps, and bones* (p. 34). New York, NY: Bloomsbury.

Chick, N. (2013). *Metacognition*. Nashville, TN: Vanderbilt University Center for Teaching. Retrieved from https://cft. vanderbilt.edu/guides-sub-pages/metacognition/. Accessed on April 19, 2021.

Laozi (approximately 516 B.C.). *Tao Te Ching*. Retrieved from https://www.5000yan.com/8.html. Accessed on May 2, 2021.

Ma, Y. (2021). *UConn music lesson*. Posted by Shao, S. on April 4. Retrieved from https://www.youtube.com/watch? app=desktop&v=835UT5V2hFc. Accessed on May 2, 2021.

Pinto, S. (2018). Intercultural competence in higher education: Academics' perspectives. *On the Horizon*, 26(2), 137–147. doi:10.1108/OTH-02-2018-0011

Rifkin, J. (2011). *The third industrial revolution: How lateral power is transforming energy, the economy, and the world*. London: Palgrave Macmillan.

Say, R. (2016). *Managing with aloha: Bringing Hawai's universal values to the art of business*. Waikoloa, HI: Ho'ohana Publishing.

Su, S. (1084). On the wall of Western Forest. Retrieved from https://www.shicimingju.com/225.html. Accessed on May 2, 2021.

Section 2

EXPERIENCES OF ESTEEMED AND YOUNG SCHOLARS

3

LIFE LESSONS FOR ASPIRING INTERNATIONAL ACADEMICS: WHAT MY EXPERIENCE SUGGESTS ABOUT HOW TO THRIVE

Vijay Kumar

ABSTRACT

I worked as an academic in Malaysia prior to taking on a similar position at a research-intensive university in New Zealand. In this chapter, I discuss challenges I faced in the early stages of my career. I provide insights into my academic mobility strategies, adapting to a research-focused environment, understanding academic standards, becoming a prolific researcher/writer, transitioning to be a 'slow' academic and finally the pursuit of striving for work-life balance. I also share my success stories with a view that these would be of benefit to aspiring international academics.

Keywords: Academic mobility; academic life; academic career; academic career advice; lived experiences; Malaysia

INTRODUCTION

I started my career in Malaysia as a teacher in a primary vernacular school and taught at the secondary and matriculation levels prior to becoming a university language teacher. The shutting down of the matriculation centre at the university meant that I had to move to the faculty level, where I was appointed as a lecturer. The university required all lecturers to have a PhD and I was lucky to be offered a scholarship to pursue my PhD in Applied Linguistics at the University of Otago in New Zealand. I served my mandatory 6-year contract and opted for optional retirement, when I was offered a full-time position at my current university in New Zealand.

The following sections provide insights into my academic challenges and opportunities in a Malaysian university. These accounts are based on my own *lived experiences* and those in the revelations of Malaysian academics whom I have met in public and private universities. The lived experiences refer to my own experiences, choices and factors that influenced my personal perceptions and interpretations.

ACADEMIC CULTURE AND FREEDOM

Institutions have their own work cultures, and some cultures provide rich developmental opportunities. My experience after completing my PhD and returning to the university in Malaysia meant that I had to adapt to an existing departmental culture. I was appointed as an academic, but I was an academic *civil servant* who did not enjoy much academic freedom. My experience was that the faculty/department predominantly dictated life, both in and out of the work environment. For example, Departmental WhatsApp groups, initially established for faster communication, are misused, with messages pouring in throughout the day including after work hours. Staff respond reactively in fear; they know that they will be reprimanded if they do not respond to text messages even when these arrive late at night. As a result of this, I missed out on a lot of private and family time as it was difficult to schedule and keep promises. There were too many ad-hoc requests, (actually directives) that disrupt teaching, research and personal time.

What this meant for me was that it was impossible to schedule research time as interruptions were 'epidemic' to say the least. Most of my research had to be conducted outside normal working hours or weekends, disrupting my work-life balance. Protected research time was not institutionalised.

The lessons I have learned from my experience in Malaysia is that there are things that can be changed and there are things that cannot be changed, and in between there is a door. The only way to survive (not thrive) is to protect your own personal time as much as you can by 'switching off' after office hours. I realised that it was MY responsibility to look after myself.

Upon reflection, I realised that the academic cultures dominated with power can be extremely harmful for any academic. In my case, I decided to swim to a new shore; one on which I would be liberated and experience being a true university academic.

CULTURAL HIERARCHIES AND THE PURSUIT OF FREEDOM

For me to land on a new shore, I had to be prepared to be accepted. While I was still in Malaysia, I knew that I had to benchmark my academic identity with that of world-class universities to gain visibility and recognition. The first thing I did was to build a niche area of research – I chose to focus on

doctoral supervision, even though my PhD was in Applied
Linguistics. This change in field was not well received or
supported by the department which did not value supervision
as a discipline even though supervision takes place in all
departments. Researching into the practice of doctoral
supervision and to provide research informed evidence for
practice was not something that was intelligible to many.
Thus, I had to seek a supportive and influential ally. The dean
of the graduate school in the Malaysian university, who later
became the vice chancellor (VC), was instrumental in
providing me with possibilities to conduct frequent support
programmes for postgraduate students and doctoral supervisors. This enabled me to research and publish into the practice. I am reminded of what a student once told me: 'It is not
who you know that is important in academia but who knows
you that matters'. Getting the VC on my side was strategic,
getting a VC who shared similar ideas was a blessing. Subsequently, I initiated an institution-wide support programme
(called *Putra Sarjana*) that gained international recognition.
My research into doctoral education, done collaboratively
with international experts in the field of doctoral education,
provided me with the avenues to reach a wider audience with
increased citations of my publications in highly ranked
doctoral education journals. This recognition led to an invitation to become a founding member of the International
Doctoral Education Network (IDERN). I chaired an IDERN
biennial meeting in Malaysia and this resulted in the Malaysian Ministry of Education commissioning me to write a
handbook on doctoral supervision for all Malaysian universities which is core supervision training manual, even now.
During my time in Malaysia, I travelled to New Zealand
frequently and I offered research-informed workshops regularly and voluntarily for postgraduates and supervisors. I also
offered research seminars in the department in which I was

planning to gain a lectureship. I also collaborated and published strategically on doctoral education research with my IDERN colleagues.

Academic mobility requires you to focus on a niche area that is in demand; it should also be one you are passionate about. I chose doctoral education as I saw a need to improve practices – this field was under-developed both in Malaysia and New Zealand. My research collaborations with international experts increased my visibility and enhanced my credibility. My close networking with top supportive academic managers in both countries was of immense value when I applied for a permanent job in New Zealand. With positive teaching evaluations, evidence of the impact of my teaching, an outstanding record of citations of my research and my international networking, I presented myself as the ideal candidate to my potential employers in New Zealand.

ADAPTING TO A NEW RESEARCH-FOCUSED ENVIRONMENT

When I was appointed in New Zealand (NZ), I was already an associate professor in Malaysia. However, I was not burdened with excessive teaching due to my seniority when I started my academic career in NZ. NZ university policies stipulate that I should not be inundated with teaching or administrative responsibilities for at least a year to enable me to settle in and to develop my networks and new research. This was also the time for me to become accustomed to the university and department culture. My confirmation goals were to publish four journal articles over 3–5 years. My confirmation reports were monitored by the Head of Department (HoD) and the Deputy Vice Chancellor, Academic (DVC(A)). In the past, I had never had any contact with a DVC(A) with regards my academic career, but here at Otago, the DVC(A) reads my confirmation reports and provides support if necessary. It is always a pleasure to read her individualised comments that appreciate the work I do. Comments such as 'I am pleased that you are an outstanding role model and ambassador of the university', coming from the DVC(A), are inspiring and motivating. To assist me with new research, I was also given substantial research funds, and I worked with a mentor whom I chose. What was unique to me in Otago was that I was allowed to have one research day per week and this research day was protected – in other words, I did not have to attend to any non-research-related tasks and could work from home on my research day. To me, this was a new understanding of what being in a research university means – my boundaries were protected institutionally to contribute to my growth as a researcher.

A point to note is that if you want to thrive in academia, your focus must be on research, and you must either be in a supportive research environment or you need to create one yourself. There also has to be balance between work and life or you will be burnt out. Two strategies I found useful were first, to seek a mentor and second, I allocated and defended my time. I chose a mentor, who was at the professorial level – he was my role model. I wanted to access his accumulated knowledge, expertise and wisdom. My mentor energised me with encouragement, support and formative feedback. He facilitated my academic success and professional development by providing insights into the expectations and working strategically in my new work environment. I allocated time to prepare and schedule my activities. I protected not only my research time but also my personal time. I allocated time for teaching, research, professional learning and also to build relationships with colleagues. Additionally, I also protected my evening and weekends in advance. I ensured that I did not take work home as that would have been disrespectful to my family. Administrators will always give you plenty of work to do; at times, there is no running away from these responsibilities, unless you are in an environment that safeguards your research time. There will always be numerous distractions and demands; it is said that time flies, but YOU are the navigator. If you do not allocate time and protect it, you will forever remain the victim. But having said that, as seen in my narrative earlier, in some institutions, your time belongs to the masters, and you are their academic puppet! What worked for me in Malaysia was to be in the office an hour early every day and start with research/writing. I did the *heavy lifting* first thing in the morning – that gave me the mental sense of accomplishment before I drowned myself in the mundane tasks of the day. If you are planning on a successful research career, bear in mind that you are responsible for your own research progress, irrespective of whether you obtain institutional support or not. In my case, I had monthly 'helicopter times' – that is time for me self-reflect on my goals particularly in terms of my career goals and work-life balance. I roped in colleagues who were prolific and proactive into my research teams so that I was motivated by their enthusiasm to produce work of international standards.

UNDERSTANDING ACADEMIC STANDARDS

I have learned that your international standing as an academic depends very much on the expected standards of the university and the academic promotion system. The academic promotion process is very different across the two institutions that I have worked for. In the university in Malaysia, specific criteria were made available – this was good, as the academic then knows exactly which boxes to tick to be promoted. It was a transparent reward system. For example, academic staff needed to obtain a minimum of 80 points to be eligible to apply to be an associate professor. Points are given for every activity that an academic undertakes. For example, one point is given for being a committee member of a task force. Points are also given for reviewing journal articles, conference attendance, being a conference chair, graduating students, gaining research funds and for publications in highly ranked journals. Academic staff must tabulate all these points and then attach evidence on each for the promotion. When I applied for a promotion to associate professor in Malaysia, I had a bound document of about 325 pages! I needed to have graduated a master's student and have published 15 journal articles. On the contrary, the criteria in the NZ University are completely different – my Malaysian associate professor status was not considered as par, and I was offered only a senior lecturer position. I was told that I was an *institutional* associate professor in Malaysia and not an associate professor of the discipline. What does this mean? This took some time to decipher! When I finally decided to apply for my promotion to associate professor in New Zealand, I was advised to have at least 35 journal articles in quality-assured international journals with a record of at least 600 citations to my credit. I was able to achieve this within 4 years due to the supportive institutional environment. I had to write a compelling three-page case for my promotion – one page each for research, teaching and service. I needed to provide evidence of sustained leadership and international recognition across all three aspects. Five independent international referee reports were taken into consideration to verify my peer recognition and international standing in the field of doctoral supervision. I remember my HoD telling me, 'If you are an associate professor here at Otago, you can give a talk in Oxford (which I did), and you will be respected!' With these high standards and achievements, my confidence as an academic grew and I began to be respected and valued more internationally.

The key message from my success here at Otago is that you must know what your goal post is. All universities have different promotion criteria; find out what these are and work towards these goals. Being an institutional associate professor may be the right pathway if that is what you want to decide as your final academic goal. However, if you want to be recognised as world class in your expertise, you need to benchmark with international standards. It might be wise to compare your achievements with institutions elsewhere so that when you become a professor, for example, you are in fact a professor of the discipline who will be revered internationally.

BECOMING A PROLIFIC RESEARCHER/WRITER

The opportunities I am given to be a prolific writer and researcher are generous in my current working environment. As indicated earlier, besides protected research/writing time, the department culture supports individuals proactively and ensures that each academic is provided the right support to grow and develop. The department has a very strong research culture. We have weekly research seminars where we present our work in progress and seek feedback – there are times when we listen to a postgraduate student who is struggling with an aspect of research, and we offer suggestions. We assist colleagues by reading their drafts of journal articles and providing constructive feedback. In addition, when our postgraduate students are preparing for an oral examination, we support them and provide input as to how they can respond to examiner comments. Thus, what is unique is that the department culture is one that is collective and formative – we play a developmental role to support each other. Hierarchy is hardly the order of the day; collegiality predominates. We also celebrate successes regularly to encourage and motivate each other. Everyone in the department makes it a point to attend research seminars to support one another – this research time is protected by the department as no other activities are organised during these times.

What is unique in this NZ University is that we have numerous writing support groups. These groups meet regularly to marshal ideas, to collaborate on research or even just to meet and provide emotional support to each other. We also have what is called the *shut up and write* groups in the department, where dedicated time is allocated for both academics and postgraduates to meet in a seminar room and do some writing together. The premise for the shut up and write groups is that writing is a social activity and writing with others in the same space encourages and motivates one to be prolific and pro-ductive. I have also teamed up with another colleague to write in a café on a regular basis. Writing in different spaces with colleagues helped me progress my research projects.

The key message from my success here in Otago is that research and writing need not be done in isolation. There are some who are productive and prolific when writing in isola-tion but if this becomes a struggle, consider joining dedicated writing groups and teaming up with supportive colleagues to whom you can be accountable. Seek proactive, supportive colleagues to travel with on your academic journey. Organise writing/research sessions with supportive and proactive col-leagues, not ones who have become complacent.

BEING A SLOW ACADEMIC

Identifying with 'busyness' is something I associate with my previous job in Malaysia; everyone was kept busy and at times it seemed to be a fashion statement. The notion was that if you were not busy, then you were not working. I used to be in a similar boat, and at the end of the day I was totally exhausted – this had an impact on my productivity as a researcher. At times, I asked myself if I had to do all those tasks and wondered if I should have prioritised – but then, priorities go out the window when management disrupts your schedule.

I was pleasantly relieved to find that this identification with busyness is not the norm in my present university. I first came across the notion of the Slow Professor when a colleague spoke about slow pedagogy in a department seminar. In essence, the Slow Professor draws on the idea that when we are rushed, we are simply not the people we are capable of being. As seen from the work culture in my previous institution, academic life is compromised when we speed up the clock with demands such as graduating on time, publishing xx number of articles and 'Mcdonaldising' doctoral supervision, that is being forced to supervise large number of students. There is no time to pause and reflect; rather, one has to enter into the mass production mode to meet ranking requirements at the expense of the well-being of staff and students. University leaders seem to have forgotten that time management is not about jamming an abundance of things into the day but rather taking out as much as possible so that we are able to produce work of high quality.

I am glad that I now have the luxury to say that most of my creativity in fact came out of my 'wasted time!' I do not do more than three tasks a day, but each of the three is done to a very high standard, which is reflective of my mastery. I do not 'get busy' for the sake of being busy. I do not confuse activity with productivity. I also go for midday walks around campus with my colleagues to recharge myself and reflect. Without this sort of reflection and slowing down, the rat race will wear us down sooner than we anticipate.

WORK-LIFE BALANCE

My conversations with academic colleagues indicate that in some environments, many are seeking help for mental health issues – many are depressed and burnout rates are high. The notion of private time, after hours or on the weekend, does not exist for some academics in some cultures simply because their private time is controlled. People in power making excessive demands throughout the day are not unheard of. If you are a person in power and send a text or email to a junior staff member, that junior is likely to be intimidated and feel the need to respond immediately out of fear of repercussions. Most academic staff work beyond normal working hours because their normal working hours are usually not within their own control. I had to adapt, and took breaks whenever I could to recuperate from burnout. In the past, during the weekends, I had to continue work as I received work-related text messages. In my current working environment, it is the exact opposite. I have been in this institution for more than 10 years now and my HoD or line managers have never contacted me on my personal phone. We do not have WhatsApp group chats; we are scheduled academics; everything is planned and thus there are no ad hoc requests from administrators – any ad-hoc requests is put into the queue. We know what specific tasks are due and when they are due. I do not receive emails after work hours and neither do I send emails to my colleagues or postgraduate students after office hours. As an international academic, my productivity is high, I feel respected and that my time is valued.

MY JOURNEY

My life at my present university is a dream for many of my academic colleagues abroad. I do not feel stressed or physically and emotionally drained. I look forward to coming to work daily, where I have the freedom to decide what to research and teach and to be selective of areas where I can contribute my expertise. I am well supported by a university that places mental health and well-being very highly and ensures my right to a private and family life. I am allowed to say NO to any institutional request and my decision is respected. I choose only to participate in committees where I can contribute. I am valued for my expertise and I am rewarded purely on the grounds of merit. I am blessed to have colleagues who are nurturing and who ensure that we are all happy in our work environment. We work at world-class levels by supporting each other and are knowledge creators. As a result of this favourable academic working environment, I think I have been exponentially successful in building my niche area; that is, doctoral supervision. I have been invited to deliver professional development programmes in 46 universities in 23 countries. I am the first person outside the United Kingdom to have become a UK Council of Graduate Education recognised doctoral supervisor. This triumph is attested to the initial support from my graduate school in Malaysia and subsequently from my present university.

These lived accounts of my experience working in two environments are not meant to show that one place is better than the other, but rather, to draw out concerns that need to be addressed. I had to experience change to grow. I have shared my lived experience of having been an academic in Malaysia, where it can be challenging to strive and thrive due to existing traditions in some departments. I have also shown that opportunities are available to any academic, but departmental and institutional cultures may stifle growth and progress and act as barriers because of the abuse of hierarchical power structures.

I have also shown that under traditions such as those I experience in New Zealand, opportunities and strategies are in place so that the academic is supported to reach for the stars. The collegial nature of working relationships is worth endeavouring for. Working environments should bring out the 'primal genius' in every academic. Additionally, I note that most academics who struggle are not strategic but reactive. My colleagues in New Zealand seem to be highly intentional – in other words, they intentionally schedule their days to reap the greatest benefits, and have a greater awareness of what is needed to contribute in their academic career, not only for their own sake but also for those around them and their field.

All great thinkers are initially ridiculed – and eventually revered.

4

MY ACADEMIC PATH AS AN INTERNATIONAL ACADEMIC FROM MENA TO CANADA: GOOD, BETTER, BEST. NEVER LET IT REST

Jinan Issa

ABSTRACT

The path to academic excellence is neither paved with roses nor easy; nonetheless, cautiously driving such a road has endless thrills especially when the driver is passionate about academia. This chapter intends to bring to the fore the hurdles I have been confronting in my academic path as an international scholar and a researcher in some of the Middle East and North Africa (MENA) countries, Malaysia and Canada (Global North and South institutions) for over 14 years. Hence, it mirrors my research experiences to guide Early Career Researchers (ECRs) and accentuates the importance of research culture, professional designations and networking with experts from other world knowledge bodies.

Keywords: Research culture; productivity; professional designations; Canadian experience; hurdles in academia; ECR

THE ACADEMIC PROFESSION

Imagine that you were walking on a well-lit road with clearly stated directions to nearby destinations. However, you suddenly had a strong feeling to alter your route to discover the unknown. It was a situation similar to early explorers who had a strong desire to explore the unexplored and discover the hidden treasures of remote lands. Admittedly, making up my mind was not easy because I had to sacrifice a well-paid job and a secure life. I simply turned the steering wheel of my career journey to commence driving on a newly blurred route.

Before entering academia, I held several positions related to the area of EFL (English as a Foreign Language) in two countries of the Middle East and North Africa (MENA) region where I taught students at different levels: secondary, post-secondary and university as well as a training and development centre in an oil refining company. The latter was the turning point in my career path as I decided to pursue my post-graduate studies in an apex research university in Malaysia, where I was indulged in a very engaging and well-built research environment. As a result, I commenced my academic career path and put down-to-earth my newly emerging academic dream.

This chapter highlights my observations and experiences as a full-time assistant professor in one of the MENA countries, Malaysia and Canada (Global North and South institutions).

It also sheds light on the importance of research culture and productivity. This chapter also illustrates what is known as 'the lack of Canadian experience' and the relevance of professional designations. Last but not least, the chapter exhibits a concluding paragraph to accept hurdles in academia once an Early Career Researcher (ECR) endeavours the academic path as a career.

RESEARCH CULTURE: AN OPPORTUNITY OR A BARRIER

If you are reading this section, congratulations. It simply means that you are either an ECR or considering an ECR job. Initially, it is pretty important for you to fully comprehend the big umbrella of research culture with some elements such as networking, research and development, and supporting expenditures. Based on my experiences as an international ECR in different tertiary educational institutions, I can tell that the research culture of a university, if not well-macadamised, will challenge researchers particularly ECRs. In fact, I was fortunate enough to work in two different research environments where one was an opportunity for improvement yet a real barrier in the other. The next paragraphs illustrate both experiences by providing few examples from my international experiences in Malaysia, MENA and Canada.

First and foremost, there is no doubt that an increasingly growing competition continues to exist among the world universities to be categorised as Research Universities (RUs). The names of best-performing universities and institutes are proudly pertinent as RUs. Yet, hundreds, if not thousands, are still seeking to reach the RU status: A journey to be best described as arduous that necessitates strenuous efforts to accelerate accomplishing and maintaining the alluring RU status. Henceforth, a robust and vigorous research culture environment is fundamental and strongly matters. I first witnessed these efforts to accelerate research culture in my previous position at the APEX University in Malaysia where I studied and worked later as an ECR. At my first start, I coauthored my first paper with my advisor and managed to get it published in a well-reputed journal. The paper was fully funded by the university and has been receiving a good number of citations. I still remember when I received an email, from a post-graduate candidate at the University of Maryland, the United States requesting to interview me regarding it. It was a feeling of pride and success that I had managed to internationally publish a worthy paper after only one term of doing my master's degree in Malaysia. In fact, it was a starting and an intriguing point in my academic record. It is worth mentioning that Malaysian research universities value research and innovation as documented in a published joint report by Malaysia's Ministry of Education, Elsevier, and QS Quacquarelli Symonds (2021):

> *Malaysia's Gross Expenditure on Research &*
> *Development (GERD) has increased by nearly $4*
> *billion USD to reach over $12 billion in 2018,*
> *representing 1.4% of the country's GDP in that year.*

My PhD was also fully funded by the university as I received the university fellowship and was awarded the Gold Medal in my graduation ceremony for being the most outstanding PhD candidate in education. The reward meant a lot to me and was an alluring corner in my academic record. Indeed, I owed a lot to my university who believed in its best-performing students. In 2018, I returned to my university as an academic staff in one of its research institutes. It was a really fascinating journey as I got involved in a few sponsored projects with new themes. I was learning new knowledge almost every day. That wonderful experience added a lot to me as an ECR and I would definitely like to work in such a motivating workplace environment.

Similarly, research has been prioritised in Canada. I have clearly evidenced tremendous research efforts and expenditures first-hand as an active ECR job seeker. Not only Canadian top research universities but also governmental agencies and other institutions actively hire researchers and research associates to facilitate their current short-term and long-term research projects. The Federal Government of Canada highly values the role of research in elevating the rank of Canadian universities. Thus, more than CAD$10 billion have been allocated to research and science since 2016 (Government of Canada, 2021). The Federal Government of Canada does not only directly provide research grants but also allocates around CAD$3 billion to renovate and upgrade labs and infrastructure. There are some other external sources for funding represented by provincial governments, businesses, not-for-profit organisations, and others. A published report in 2011 mentioned that 38.2% of Canada's Research and development was allocated to research in 2010 (AUCC, 2011). Accordingly, Canada's investment in high-quality research to solve the emerging crises has reaped a lot of successes as witnessed in its prestigious research universities and the latest harvest can be seen in the promising Canadian-based COVID-19 vaccine 'Medicago' (Medicago, 2021).

Currently, in Canada, I am not working as an academic staff member, instead I registered to study as a local student for a second career in Fashion Marketing and Management as it is fully sponsored by the Government of Canada and the Government of Ontario. I am looking forward to studying a different major to get new knowledge and practical skills in this area. I am here advising ECRs to never stop learning especially about new knowledge and fields to never get left behind in our fast-changing world. If you have a dream, work hard to make it a reality and think about how you can link it to the big network of research.

Nonetheless, a quality research environment constitutes a real constraint in some, if not many, Middle East universities. Based on my experience, academic staff were loaded with long teaching and office hours but financially supporting research was hardly available to encourage research activities; for example, publications. On the contrary, conducting research, updating research skills and sponsoring publications were mostly individual initiatives. Unfortunately, the university's top management did not prioritise research and publications when I was there. Only very recently, academics were asked to record their research achievements at the end of each academic semester due to academic accreditation for institutional programmes by the Academic Accreditation Authority. Research grants have also become available for researchers to apply despite a few constraints related to technical issues such as not clearly stating the must-have documents on the related webpage on submitting research proposals. I personally encountered this challenge only a few months ago when a worthy research proposal did not see the light for the above-mentioned reason. I used 'worthy' to describe the project proposal based on the reviewers' evaluations and comments. Luckily after appealing, the project proposal will be considered for the next opening call. It is worthy to mention, there have been some efforts, in establishing a research council to facilitate and financially sponsor academic and industrial research proposals.

Accordingly, a fruitfully paved research environment is the platform that expedites research projects. On the contrary, the research environment can be challenging and constitutes a real obstacle in some tertiary institutions. I encountered such an obstacle, as explained earlier, and tried to overcome it by following some tips; For example, participating in local and international conferences, networking with local and international ECRs in other universities, and co-authoring research papers, especially with colleagues located in other countries. On the other hand, tertiary institutions should encourage the teamwork of small research groups and promote themes for emerging research topics that can inspire ECRs. Equally important, running professional development workshops about the latest statistical packages to analyse quantitative and qualitative research, for instance, ATLAS-ti, SmartPLS and AMOS, as well as research methodologies and designs can guide many ECRs in their research. Hence, providing such supports advocates cross-disciplinary thinking, advances collaborative research activities with experts in the field and ultimately elevates research culture to be seen as an opportunity and not as a constraint. Finally, yet importantly, I hope that all tertiary institutions prioritise robust research culture and invest in building a productive research environment through providing support to inspire ECRs to be prolific researchers.

PRODUCTIVITY: A CURSE OR BLESSING

In academia, there is an intense urge to be productive in terms of research and publications. I felt the utmost experience when I worked in Malaysia. Nonetheless, there is the uncomfortable feeling of not doing enough especially when some of my prolific colleagues celebrate their ongoing achievements of being noticed and received the lights of fame for receiving awards on their publications in highly reputed journals and prestigious book publishing.

Undeniably, fostering quality research environments and providing various supports to encourage conducting research are the most significant contributors to research productivity in academia on two levels: individual (ECR) and institutional (university). This sturdy relationship positively drives research productivity. To make sure this significant relation occurs and sees the light, academicians and institutions ought to prioritise research productivity and make it their top agenda. Tertiary institutions ought to clearly demonstrate research goals and strongly empower staff to be involved in funded projects. Providing funds plays a pivotal role in attracting academicians to increase their research productivity. I know it is not easy to provide capital to sponsor research activities especially when some economies are not powerful enough or fully dependent on the prices of some materials; for example, oil. I still remember when the prices of oil sharply dropped, all research-related expenditures in Oman were cut down as a result of that decrease. Research activities were not exceptions. Thus, tertiary institutions should always seek extra sources for funding and not mainly depend on their government central-ised budgets, especially public institutions.

From the individual lens, each ECR should build his or her network and actively team up with other ECRs creating small teams to work on research projects. Team members may vary to include graduates from different universities. This strategy assists in sharing existing knowledge, solving emerging problems together and updating research skills as well as ultimately contributing to the international universities through patents. Indeed, positiveness should feature the research teams' climates to share positive attitudes, an effec-tive communicative language, and spread a spirit of cooper-ation by empowering 'together we can make it'. Accordingly, professional, friendly and decent practices would govern the relationship between/among team members to promote and facilitate research productivity. Moreover, team members should actively seek local and international grants to sponsor their research activities. I personally co-authored research with my Omani colleagues and submitted it to The Research Council (TRC) to obtain funding. TRC in Oman is not only open to local ECRs but international ECRs from all over the world. Time management is another relevant element to consider when productivity is the target. Every ECRs should prioritise tasks and plan their agendas in accordance with due dates. That's my own strategy in accomplishing the tasks set. Certainly, academicians are like all other professionals who need to manage their time and schedule their priorities according to certain due dates. Planning and setting a due date for each task, including research and publications, is of equal priority to other academic tasks like teaching courses. By the end of each academic year, academic staff become proud of their achievements and see the blessings of being productive.

Based on the institutional lens, rewards and incentives should be provided to celebrate research success. Also, considering and emphasising the selection of only talented ECRs during recruiting new academic staff should be highlighted. When a new top talented ECR staff is employed, tertiary institutions will enhance their competitiveness and ultimately successes. Boosting research productivity becomes feasible when recruiting the right ECRs on the team. Most importantly, chairs of programmes and heads of departments had better be true leaders who inspire and encourage staff to do research. Thus, such leaders should have high research skills and are research-oriented. My advisor, a Professor in Malaysia is the best example of such a leader. I consider him as my guru who is incredibly supportive. I first met him when I was doing my master's degree in 2009 and since then he has become my role model as a course coordinator, an advisor, a co-author, a colleague, a director and a real empowering leader. I am blessed to have him in my academic journey because he has been very cooperative in providing consultations and guidance till the moment. Additionally, continuous professional development workshops are to be pre-scheduled and available for staff to register for free. Yet, outsiders should pay fees as a source of generating some income to sponsor research activities.

Why not form some research cliques to familiarise ECRs especially juniors with the prolific senior researchers? Tertiary institutions should announce certain emerging themes to study the encountering problems and suggest proper solutions. For example, Universiti Sains Malaysia made a call about different themes in marketing and branding for the university to attract more new international students. The university offered short-term grants to all academic staff to sponsor projects investigating the reasons behind the dropped numbers. Hence, tertiary institutions should lead their academic staff towards the importance of doing research, especially during critical times to serve the university, the community, the nation and the entire world. I evidenced that call when I worked as an ECR in IPPTN USM (The National Higher Education Research Institute, University Sains Malaysia). I remember that I was inspired by that call and worked on a project proposal with a senior researcher. At the same time, I co-worked on big research that was fully sponsored by the Malaysian Ministry of Higher Education and the university with the Lead Professor. It was another fabulous experience that added a lot to my knowledge and research skills.

In closing, I highly recommend facilitating research teams and cliques to accommodate diverse ECRs needs as they provide fabulous opportunities to share knowledge and update skills.

THE IMPORTANCE OF
PROFESSIONAL DESIGNATIONS

This section demonstrates the importance of professional designations to sustain a job in the Canadian job market whether in academia or any sector. I have encountered the challenge of not getting a professional job in Canadian universities and colleges mainly because of not having the relevant professional designation. Despite the fact that all my academic international qualifications were verified and accredited by WES – Canada (World Education Services – Canada), I can say that I evidenced closed doors to be employed in Canadian universities especially to get a tenure-track position.

Let me begin by clarifying what a professional designation means. It refers to a title as an acronym issued by a professional organisation to certify that you have the professional degree or skill needed for a particular job. There are certain requirements that each applicant should complete to be eligible to apply for a particular professional designation. Once a professional designation is issued to an applicant, it demonstrates the degree of excellence evidenced as a stamped title next to your name in your curriculum vitae or resume and your LinkedIn professional page. Such designations open closed doors for their holders in the same state or province and/or other states or provinces. In addition, some professional designations are valid to be used internationally. Examples are OCELT (Ontario Certified English Language Teacher), PMP (Project Management Professional), OMVIC (Ontario Motor Vehicle Industry Council) and CPA (Chartered Professional Accountant).

Most, if not all, professional designations and certifications necessitate further study after the undergraduate degree plus receiving some training as a practical experience from accredited organisations. A dedicated candidate can get the professional designation, in some cases, even without travelling to the country where a particular professional organisation is located especially after the spread of asynchronous and synchronous learning. In Canada, having a professional designation is a must to get a professional job. For instance, if a newcomer has some international experience in working as a car salesman before immigrating to Canada; he/she needs to be OMVIC certified to work in the same profession in Ontario. In other words, without the OMVIC certification, you will not get a chance to work in any car dealership in Ontario regardless of your expertise. Likewise, an ESL (English as a Second Language) instructor needs to be licensed and certified as an OCELT to continue in the same career in Ontario and other provinces in Canada. I can say that professional designations are the keys to impress recruiters and hiring managers in Canada. The academic job market is not an exception. I noticed when I was applying for academic jobs that there was a section for licenses and certifications. I used to neglect it as I mistakenly thought that it cannot be as important as my academic qualifications. However, I soon realised that I was wrong. The more licences and certifications I have, the more opportunities I have to be accepted.

Therefore, if you think about moving to Canada, my advice would be to start searching for your desired professional designation and certification as well as the related professional association, which issues the targeted professional designation to save time and start the process of training and testing and any other requirements needed. You can also apply to get multiple professional designations to increase your marketability and impress recruiters. Finally, remember that you can start this process from any location in the world. Do not delay things to a later stage especially about elevating your study or profession.

LACK OF CANADIAN EXPERIENCE

This section represents the other main hurdle to get an academic job in Canadian universities and colleges. There is a crystal clear truth that you cannot get a job in academia without having a Canadian reference. So, I highlight the importance of having a Canadian experience or reference in this section. 'Lack of Canadian experience' often refers to the lack of appropriate soft skills needed for a particular job. It can also be interpreted that the candidate is not a good fit for a particular job due to the cultural norms of the Canadian marketplace and some related work ethics. Once a newcomer arrives in Canada and starts the process of searching for a professional job, the applicant will hear from the officially registered employer counsellor about the importance of having the Canadian experience in the job market for the tremendous role it plays to facilitate getting a job.

There is some sort of consensus among most hiring managers and employers that the Canadian workplace culture challenges most, if not all, newcomers. Although it is a subjective touchstone, it exists in reality as I was told by my officially registered employment advisors. So, I will tackle some recommendations, based on my experience, below to overcome the crucial obstacle of 'lack of Canadian experience':

- Register at one of the employment agencies in your city. There are some non-for-profit employment agencies, which receive funding either from the Federal Government of Canada or the governments of provinces. Because I live in London, Ontario, I am familiar with the employment agencies located in London. To mention some: WIL Employment Connections, LEADS Employment Services, Goodwill Career Centre and Access Centre for Regulated

Employment. After you land in your city, search for such employment agencies to register with one. After your registration, you will have an employment counsellor.

- Make sure that you get the accreditation of all your international academic qualifications from WES – Canada (Word Education Service – Canada) if you have not done the verification yet.

- Your employment counsellor will register you for a training workshop delivered by a Certified Résumé Strategist about the techniques of writing a well-tailored resume and a cover letter. You can receive other services like mentorship. You can also learn some tips to succeed in an interview by a Certified interview Strategist. Your career advisor and a coach will guide and assist you till you get hired.

- Work on your professional designation(s) to enhance your marketability.

- It is important to volunteer to gain your Canadian experience and enrich your hands-on experience. It is more preferable if you volunteer in a desirable organisation. In other words, you should do your unpaid volunteer opportunities for an organisation or a company where you hope to be recruited.

- Building professional connections is foremost to open locked doors in the Canadian marketplace, which is also applicable in academia. It can be done through knowing new people and taking the initiative to volunteer in community centres or university projects. You can get a reference which is essential to facilitate your employment opportunity. References are your master keys. Without their endorsement, your job application is likely to be neglected at the early stage of screening applications.

- Update your LinkedIn profile by adding your skills, certificates, experiences, projects, volunteering opportunities and connections. If you have not got a LinkedIn page, create your page immediately and use it actively. Engage in discussions and connect with experts in your area like mentors. Register with TRIEC Mentoring Partnership, in the Toronto region, and IMMPLOY, in London, Ontario, for mentor or mentee opportunities.

- Register yourself for an OSLT (Occupation-Specific Language Training) course or ELT (English Language Training) courses which are funded by Immigration, Refugees and Citizenship Canada for permanent residents and refugees. OSLT course assists newcomers to break the language barrier.

ACCEPTING HURDLES IN ACADEMIA

The academic profession has many alluring sides yet can be arduous. Throughout my ongoing academic journey, I have always been motivated and guided by St. Jerome's quote 'Good, better, best. Never let it rest. Til the good is better and the better is best'. It is worth mentioning that tenured academics reap the advantages of financial reliability and job security compared to contracted academics. Nonetheless, long-term contracted academics enjoy numerous benefits, which can include but are not limited to: well-paid salaries; annual return tickets; furnished or semi-furnished accommodation; medical health insurance; paid annual vacation; end-of-service gratuity; and even sometimes subsidisedschooling for up to two children. What is more, tenured academics are favoured with pension and long-term research grants.

However, the current academic job market offers limited tenure-track positions. As a result, academicians are vying for those vacancies. A competition, if anything to be described, not easy at all. After the long and tiring journey of getting a PhD degree in a particular specialisation, you confront numerous hurdles to start climbing, if not yet, the academic ladder. Bryan Gopaul, a panel member in the Council of Canadian Academies and an academic staff at the University of Rochester, describes the academic situation of PhD holders in Canada searching for jobs as 'ripe for dialogue and reform' (Peters, 2021). Henceforth, there is a call for reforms in the academic job market.

To excel in academia, research culture is the key plus the power of accepting encountered hurdles. As an ECR, you need to acquire some soft skills after you get your PhD qualification and achieve your professional designation(s). Additionally, you should be open to new cultures and improve your connections. Building your professional network is of extreme importance to engaging in new projects and collaborating with international professionals. Senior researchers always emphasise that a genuine camaraderie on academic teams facilitates the production of worthy research especially when networking is enabled and highly encouraged with other academicians in the same area and other related areas to make beautifully knitted articles, which are meant to be shared to contribute to the existing knowledge.

Actively seek new connections and references to sustain your academic position simply because most jobs in academia are hidden. In fact, connections or references facilitated my academic journey, in particular, as I am a determined ECR who is willing to jump into new projects and always takes the initiative with great verbal and written communication skills. It is also highly recommended to improve your administrative, time management and organisational skills. Last but not least, be supportive, professional and proactive with top-notch computer skills and research skills.

REFERENCES

AUCC (Association of Universities and Colleges of Canada). (2011). The value of university research. Retrieved from https://www.univcan.ca/wp-content/uploads/2011/10/the-value-of-university-research-oct-2011.pdf

Government of Canada. (2021). Canada's science vision. Retrieved from https://www.ic.gc.ca/eic/site/131.nsf/eng/home

Malaysia's Ministry of Education, Elsevier, & QS Quacquarelli Symonds. (2021). Malaysia's R&D investment paying off with higher research productivity and improved university ranking. Retrieved from https://www.elsevier.com/about/press-releases/corporate/malaysias-r-and-d-investment-paying-off-with-higher-research-productivity-and-improved-university-ranking#:~:text=A%20joint%20report%20by%20Malaysia's%244%20billion%20USD%20to%20reach

Medicago. (2021). COVID-19 vaccine development program. Retrieved from https://www.medicago.com/en/covid-19-programs/

Peters, D. (2021, January 27). The mismatch continues between PhD holders and their career prospects. *University Affairs in Canada*. Retrieved from https://www.universityaffairs.ca/news/news-article/the-mismatch-continues-between-phd-holders-and-their-career-prospects/

5

BEING AN INTERNATIONAL ACADEMIC IN A MALAYSIAN UNIVERSITY: CHALLENGES, OPPORTUNITIES AND WAY FORWARD

Muhammad Muftahu

ABSTRACT

In the Malaysia National Higher Education Strategic Plan 2007–2020 and Malaysia Education Blueprint (Higher Education) 2015–2025, the country plans to become one of the international education hubs across the globe. One of the critical strategies is to increase the diverse number of international academics in Malaysian tertiary institutions. As an outcome of strategic initiatives derived from the blueprint, Malaysia has continuous recruitment of international academics in the country's universities. Against this background, this chapter will discuss my experiences as an international academic from Nigeria in a research institute in a Malaysian university. I will relate a few personal and professional issues and challenges that encountered in the course of my service in

*the country. I will then propose some practical sugges-
tions to overcome these challenges.*

Keywords: International; academics; research institute;
Malaysia; Nigeria; academic promotion

MY BACKGROUND AND DIVERSE
ACADEMIC JOURNEY

I am a citizen of the Federal Republic of Nigeria, located in
Western Africa and is recognised as the most populous across
the African continent (Muhammad, 2021). Nigeria is known
as one of the fastest-growing economies in Africa. In 2018, the
country had an estimated total population of 199,441,213
(Muhamad, 2021). In terms of education, the federal government offers free universal basic education and subsidises
higher education fees in public institutions. There are 191
universities, comprising 44 federal universities, 48 state universities and 99 private universities (National Universities
Commission, 2021), thus making the Nigerian Higher Education system the biggest in Africa (Muhammad, 2021).

My journey towards becoming an academic in Malaysia
began with my decision to study PhD in the country. After
getting National Certificate of Education and Bachelor of
Education in Nigeria, I obtained my master's degree from an
Australian university. Then I decided to enrol in Universiti
Sains Malaysia (USM) for my PhD, which I received in 2016.
After my graduation, I worked in Saudi Arabia for about two
years before being extended an invitation to work with the
National Higher Education Research Institute (NAHERI),

USM, which I gladly joined in June 2018. At the time of my appointment, one other international academic is working at the institute.

Generally, my role is to contribute to the internationalisation of the university's research excellence and extend its global network and reputation. At the time of my first appointment, in reality, however, my primary responsibility is consistent with what is known as 'Type 2B international academics' (Da Wan & Morshidi, 2018) – junior staff who are expected to produce research papers for ranking purposes and promoting university's internalisation agenda. I have no teaching responsibilities except for providing training series for postgraduate students and supervision. However, since I joined the institute each semester I am invited as a guest lecturer for a number of courses from school of educational studies at master's and doctoral level. In other words, the research institute assigned me primarily a research-only role. This ranking-oriented expectation is not uncommon among universities in Malaysia. As will be shared in the following sections, such expectation and being assigned a research-only role has vast implications.

BEING A MALAYSIAN INTERNATIONAL ACADEMIC

These days, international academics in Malaysian universities are no longer a tiny minority. For example, at my current university, many come from somewhere other than Malaysia. And this is a typical picture in many universities around the country.

Working as an international academic is a mutually beneficial affair, bringing a range of benefits to academia and the hiring institution. International academics can enhance students' experience linguistically and culturally and bring competitive advantages and esteem to the institutions. In addition, the academics' home country knowledge and contacts can also be beneficial to the institutions. Likewise, international academics can look forward to enriching their own linguistic and cultural experiences and getting recognition as international scholars. They can also learn about the host country's local knowledge and expand their networks.

In my case, working as an international academic in a research position comes with several advantages that can turn into great opportunities. To begin with, I was able to be exposed to research at an early stage of my career. As a result, I have conducted extensive research both at local and international levels. In addition, the research projects have provided me with opportunities to create a vast network with scholars and policymakers within Malaysia and internationally.

From the grants that I received from the Malaysian government and the Nigerian government, I had the opportunity to participate in several research projects on higher education for my native country, Nigeria. These projects have resulted in papers, reports and policy papers at the local and international levels. All of these academic achievements can exert significant positive influences on both Malaysia and Nigeria's higher education development.

In 2019, the institute appointed me as a coordinator of Global Higher Education Network (GHEN). GHEN is a core and catalyst programme that amasses higher education experts worldwide to facilitate practical cooperation and collaboration in higher education. It was established as an international platform for networking and collaboration for educators and academicians, to discuss contemporary issues of globalisation and internalisation in higher education and to build a relationship with existing and future partner institutions in higher education. My position as a GHEN coordinator has given me further opportunities to build extensive academic network with scholars worldwide.

The institute has also tasked me to supervise several post-graduate students from various nationalities. To me, the relatively high number of students placed under my responsibility is a recognition of my academic ability in imparting and generating new knowledge. Moreover, supervising students comes with some welcomed benefits. Since my students come from different countries, I can explore new international collaborative research projects, increasing my knowledge base and expertise.

CHALLENGES OF BEING AN INTERNATIONAL ACADEMIC IN MALAYSIA FROM AFRICA

Malaysia aspires to be a competitive global higher education hub; therefore, it is essential to attract and integrate academic talents, who are inspiring, outstanding and thoughtful leaders in the Malaysian higher education system. The country must fully integrate these talents into the system to benefit from their service. At present, in Malaysian higher education institutions, most international academics are in junior positions (Lecturers, research follows, postdoctoral, and teaching fellows). The institutions hire them mainly to carry out research and publish papers so that the hiring universities can be competitive in the world ranking. This practice not only helps the universities to accelerate their rise in the ranking systems but also helps us to gain positive experiences and be recognised globally through our research projects and publications.

However, there has been a lack of initiatives to integrate international academics into higher education institutions in Malaysia, especially junior researchers in public universities. As a result, many face number of challenges. I have categorised these challenges into four main themes: cultural and linguistic difficulties, contract renewal leading to the lack of job security, immigration regulation and promotion.

Cultural and Linguistic Challenges

Integration of international academics into the local context can have profound emotional impacts on them. In my opinion, one of the effective ways to retain international academics in Malaysia is by integrating them with the country's culture, ethics and language, especially at the initial stage of their employment. Therefore, it would be desirable for the hiring universities to provide related support for international academics.

In most universities, however, there are limited initiatives to facilitate the integration. The international academics feel constrained in their institutions. They do not have gatherings to communicate with each other and learn about different cultures. They do not have an opportunity to participate in mobility programmes, especially academic exchange programmes, such as visiting and surveying other Malaysian higher education institutions to keep them updated about Malaysian higher education and academic culture. As international academics, our workloads preclude us from scholarly exchange with other scholars out of the university's campus. Personally, been from social sciences, many of my research projects focus on my home country because I have not had many opportunities to understand or explore the Malaysian academic culture to come up with ideas worthy of studying or researching.

Another challenge is language, especially the use of the national language – Bahasa Melayu – as the administrative language. The management at the most of the institutions uses the national language in official circulars. This practice presents a lot of difficulty for the international academics in comprehending and responding to the circulars. Often, we have to rely on our local colleagues to translate the documents. In my opinion, as the universities have has international academics, having an English language speaking environment, especially in official contexts, would greatly facilitate communication and enhance the efficiency of our work.

Contract Renewal Leading to the Lack of Job Security

Similar to local academics, international academics see job security as a crucial element of work. It can give us a sense of belonging and citizenship to the university. However, in reality, due to our contractual position, we lack job security. Typically, an international academics is been appointed to serve for one to three years at a time in an institution, after which their performance will be reviewed and evaluated for renewal.

A major challenge regarding the contract is its short duration. Since April 2020, Malaysian staff can gain a maximum of seven-year contract until they are promoted to associate professor. However, international staff are given a much shorter duration, which is between one and three years. As a result, we need to renew our contract frequently. At my university, a panel comprising the Deputy Vice-Chancellor and two or three Senate/Board of governor representatives decides each contract renewal.

The short duration of the contract cannot accurately reflect the nature of our academic achievements as academic achievements are not like 'fast food'. They need time and dedication. For example, one paper's publication will need at least three or four months, even half a year or more, to be published, and it cannot be completed in a short time, and a book needs one year or more to be written and published. In other words, being evaluated by the panel for contract renewal within a short duration of time raises a lot of concerns as the targets that we seek to accomplish would still be in progress.

What's more, our contract depends on our university's budget. Therefore, the renewal of our contract does not necessarily depend on our academic performance, but on the annual budget of our university. This scenario has contributed to the huge loss of excellent international staff, which can potentially severely affect the quality of teaching and research and decrease the reputation of a university.

A further issue is staff start-off package, which comprises incentives and equipment for new staff as soon as they report for duty. We, the international academic staff, are not entitled to the many incentives enjoyed by local academics such as career development programme, promotion opportunities and research support, such as obtaining laptops, which are given to newly recruited permanent staff as a start-off package. These are imperative for us to grow in our position as academics. The contract system puts international staff in a disadvantaged position, as it does not make up the missing package accorded to permanent staff.

In addition, services such as serving committees and assessing students' drafts are not counted as achievements. Yet, we may be questioned or queried for not meeting the criteria for being a student's main supervisor. Previously, as a practice, an academic was not allowed to be a main supervisor if they have not successfully graduated any student. For new international academics, such 'ruling' is problematic. Due to our short contract, it would be unlikely for us to have any graduated students. Consequently, it would be impossible for them to be appointed as a main supervisor, unless a senior colleague who has graduated students before is willing to invite them as a co-supervisor. Furthermore, the lack of possibility to be the main supervisor would impact their annual performance appraisal in terms of their supervision. Fortunately, the 'ruling' has recently been lifted.

The Immigration Regulations

As international academics, we do not face any problem in getting our visa and working permission as long as our institutions give us the official approval letter of employment. USM has been highly supportive in this matter. However, some immigration regulations are disadvantageous to international academics, especially those who bring their family with them. For example, the immigration department does not permit our spouses to work in Malaysia. Many international academics come with their families who are professionals in different educational fields, but they can utilise their expertise for economic gains due to the regulation.

We also face some problems concerning our children's education. Although we are allowed to enrol our children in national schools, we need to pay specific fees. A more significant challenge is language barrier. The language of instruction used at the schools is Malay. As they are new to the country, the children are likely to find problems in following the lessons taught at the schools due to the lack of familiarity with the national language. They also face challenges in communicating with their local peers, who mostly tend to use Malay, Chinese or Tamil languages in their communication.

A further problem pertains to residency. There are international academics who decided to work in Malaysia due to the country's religious and cultural proximity. Because of these, they are motivated to stay longer or even permanently. However, as foreign workers, we cannot get permanent residency until we have 10 years of working experience in Malaysia. Even with this length of experience, we still need a recommendation from our employer or a reputable referee to become a permanent Malaysian resident. As a result of our inability to get permanent residency, compounded by contractual restrictions, we cannot have any permanent

position in public or private universities. This problem leads
to the lack of job security.

Promotion

Malaysia has experienced a rise in foreign labour inflows in
response to steady economic expansion and demographic
changes. In recent years, the foreign workforce is around 15 to
20% of the total labour force (International Labour Organization, 2020; World Bank, 2020). In addition, a large number
of foreign workers have contributed to the Malaysian economy and culture. Thus, they deserve to receive equal treatment
as their local counterparts.

However, this is not the case in Malaysian higher education institutions generally. It is quite challenging for international academics to get promotions in the institutions.
According to Da Wan and Morshidi (2018), international
academics cannot be promoted while they are employed on a
contractual basis. Unlike Malaysian academics, they are only
eligible to be considered for promotion towards the end of
their contracts. Thus, it is not surprising that very few international academics hold top management positions in
Malaysian higher education institutions. This lack of promotion opportunities has been one of the significant sources of
frustration among international academics.

Being appointed primarily to conduct research and publish
papers can also impact our promotion opportunities. To be
considered for promotion, an academic, local and international, must carry out other responsibilities too, such as
teaching, service to the university and service to the community. This expectation puts international academics like me at
a considerable disadvantage as we either have reduced
teaching responsibilities or no teaching responsibilities at all.

Furthermore, as there are limited opportunities for us to be provided top management or leadership roles, our quantity and quality of service to the university is severely restricted.

CONCLUSION AND RECOMMENDATIONS

My experience as an international academic in Malaysia is enriching but challenging. On the one hand, I have learned a lot about the diverse cultures and languages of the people in Malaysia. I was also able to expand my networks among my Malaysian counterparts and international counterparts through the various research projects I carried out and my role as a GHEN coordinator. However, on the other hand, there are many challenges that I have to deal with, namely, cultural and linguistic difficulties, contract renewal and job insecurity, immigration regulations and restricted promotion opportunity.

Generally speaking, many other international academics in Malaysia also face these challenges. If Malaysia expects to retain and attract international academics, it is imperative that the Malaysian higher education institutions seriously address the challenges. Some recommendations that may be worth considering are presented below.

To address cultural and linguistic challenges, higher education institutions should:

1. Organise formal community gatherings
   I believe organising formal community gatherings inside our campus will allow us to be familiar with the diverse local cultures and languages. We can also have the opportunity to get to know our colleagues and other scholars inside and outside our faculty and our campus. I

think such programmes can significantly help ease our integration, give us a positive experience, and provide a conducive environment for us to work in. These in turn will benefit the country as they can attract more outstanding international academics and retain the existing ones.

2. Organise mobility programmes for international academics
   Mobility programmes involving visits to higher education institutions in Malaysia and abroad will be beneficial in enhancing our higher education knowledge and exposure. These programmes, in turn, will benefit the country as we can contribute more productively and significantly from the new experiences.

3. Promote an English speaking environment
   Effective communication at the workplace is important personally and professionally. Therefore, higher education institutions, especially public universities, should make English the medium of instruction in official matters and day-to-day office management. This practice will promote inclusivity and make international academics feel more welcomed. Lessons at schools should also be conducted in English so that our children can adapt and integrate better into the new environment.

To address the challenges related to contract renewal, the government and higher education institutions should:

1. Offer extended duration of contract to international academics
   International academics should be given a longer duration of contract so that they can accomplish their targets such as book publication and postgraduate supervision. The

extended contract can also help them be more competitive with their local counterparts in terms of promotion.

2. Implement a fair contract renewal process
Contract renewals should be merit-based, and the assessors should not disqualify an international academics for their lack of teaching responsibilities unless the responsibilities were already assigned beforehand. Instead, they should be evaluated based on the initial expectations when they signed the contract.

To address the challenges related to immigration regulations, the government should:

1. Provide our spouses with working visa
Many countries such as Australia, Denmark and Canada allow spouses or accompanying partners to work. It is therefore strongly recommended that this kind of privilege be given by the Malaysian government as well. Otherwise, international scholars may look for other opportunities in other countries.

2. Offer the right of permanent residence and citizenship
The time to get the right of permanent residence and citizenship for international academics should be shortened. Ten years or more is a long time for us as this ruling significantly impacts our job security. Worst, it will also lead to the loss of international talents for this country.

As for the challenges related to promotion, the Malaysian higher education institutions should:

1. Change its one-size-fits-all model for promotion purposes
As international academics' workload is primarily

research-based, there should be a specialised promotion pathway for us. Our promotion criteria should not be similar to those employed for local academics, which are broader, involving not just research and publication but also services and administration.

It is recommended that the Malaysian higher education institutions implement differentiated career pathways as outlined by the Ministry of Higher Education Malaysia (2016). The framework recommends four career pathways: teaching, research, professional practice and institutional leadership. I firmly believe adopting this framework would result in a fairer and more transparent assessment for promotion purposes.

2. Implement professional development programmes for international academics
   As we are highly expected to excel in research and publication, appropriate professional programmes, such as talent mobility and institutional leadership activities, should support our development. Universities should also extend incentives such as free laptops to international academics. These initiatives can significantly help us to excel and become more competitive.

3. Be more inclusive in appointing academics for top management positions
   Being allowed to serve top management duties would significantly contribute to our promotion opportunity. Perhaps, a good example to follow is the International Islamic University Malaysia, in which some of the top administrative positions such as Deputy Dean and Dean are held by international academics.

In conclusion, being an international academic in Malaysia offers me many opportunities to grow professionally and personally and the ability to contribute to the country and my home country. However, there is still a lot that the Malaysian government can do to attract and retain international academics. An inclusive and fair academic environment that is supportive and attentive to international academics' professional and personal needs can give us a more positive, integrated and pleasant working experience. It will certainly make the idea of working in Malaysia more attractive for outstanding international talents.

REFERENCES

Da Wan, C., & Morshidi, S. (2018). International academics in Malaysian public universities: Recruitment, integration, and retention. *Asia Pacific Education Review*, 19(2), 241–252.

International Labour Organization. (2020). Triangle in ASEAN quarterly briefing note. Retrieved from https://www.ilo.org/wcmsp5/groups/public/—asia/—robangkok/documents/genericdocument/wcms_614381.pdf

Ministry of Higher Education. (2016). *Strengthening academic career pathways and leadership development.* Putrajaya: Ministry of Higher Education.

Muhammad, M. (2021). The development of private higher education in Nigeria: A comparative analysis between Northern and Southern region. *International Journal of Higher Education*, 10(3), 178–186.

National Universities Commission. (2021). Nigerian universities. Retrieved from http://nuc.edu.ng/. Accessed on April, 2021.

World Bank. (2020). *Who is keeping score? Estimating the number of foreign workers in Malaysia.* Retrieved from https://openknowledge.worldbank.org/handle/10986/ 33730

6

FACETS OF ACADEMIC LIFE – PERSPECTIVE OF AN INTERNATIONAL VISITING SCHOLAR

Amrita Kaur

ABSTRACT

The ivory tower of academia is intriguing yet an interesting place to enter, survive and thrive. As an international academic who has worked in four different countries, I ground my reflections in three spheres, namely my positionality, my institutional culture and global academic culture. In this chapter, I describe how these three dimensions may sometimes collide to induce conflict yet converge at some point to create a thriving space for international academics. I share my stories and lived experiences to elaborate on my experiences of challenges and opportunities in academia and share insights for those who seek to be a part of academia.

Keywords: Academia; international academics; mobility; internationalisation; higher education; career

INTRODUCTION: INSIDE THE IVORY TOWER
ACROSS BORDERS

Academia is a venerable yet complex space and is often equated with an ivory tower, celebrated at times and criticised at times. Institutes of higher education across the globe hold wider accountability for social, economic, political and environmental impact at the local, regional, national and international levels. Amidst seen and unseen forces that shape the culture and functioning of academia, stakeholders especially academics seek ways, sometimes willingly and at times unwillingly to work in tandem with those forces to strike a balance to survive and thrive in academia. The wave of internationalisation of higher education has prompted global mobility of academics across the globe. While this thrust has opened up numerous opportunities for students and academics, it has also augmented the complexity of academia especially for 'self-dependent' early-career academics like me, which I seek to articulate in this chapter.

I use the analogy of the ivory tower to set the background especially in the context of internationalisation and academic mobility. It is to demonstrate the competencies an international academic must possess or develop and strategies they must adopt to establish a healthy connection within the academic community (the so-called ivory tower) and the communities outside of academia to prove their worth as a scholar. In the section below, I will briefly describe the three spaces, which are my positionality, institutional culture and global academic culture, and describe how elements of three of these spaces come together to provide opportunities and challenges. In the section, I narrate how I navigate through those opportunities and challenges and shape my academic identity.

POSITIONALITY

Identifying and articulating my positionality about who I am and where I am coming from is essential for defining my worldview specifically about how I interpret my journey as an international academic. Not everyone begins their professional careers in academia; several individuals make this shift from industry to academia at different stages of their professional lives, thus making that period a critical component of your academic journey. Interestingly, the institution of one's postgraduate qualification, its policies, the supervisory support and students support services and even the subject area of doctoral research function as critical factors in determining your academic journey. After all, those experiences lay foundations for individuals to begin the construction of their academic identity.

I was born and raised in India and after accomplishing my bachelor's and master's degree, I moved to Thailand to be a school teacher. I had been an educator for 12 years in two different countries – India and Thailand. Then I decided to pursue my doctoral studies in educational psychology at a reputed public university in Malaysia from 2007 to 2011. I was working as the head of school at a Thai bilingual school in Bangkok. I was fortunate to be able to choose my doctoral research topic based on my work experience and personal interest. This helped me pursue my thesis with extreme interest and dedication. I was also privileged to be supervised by an acclaimed supervisor who had extensive experience in my area of study. My doctoral university also offered impressive infrastructure, students support facilities, and policies that offered me numerous opportunities to train myself as a researcher and an academic and provided conducive social and academic support through peers.

An important question that should precede this discussion is what lies behind the pursuit of obtaining a doctoral qualification. While some aim to continue in academia to teach and research, others wish to bring their training to industries or corporations to maximise their output. Nevertheless, for those who choose to continue in academia, their doctoral journey serves as a stepping stone. Although it is sometimes challenging to achieve that clarity, it is advisable to give serious thought to what will follow upon the completion of the doctoral degree.

In my case, I had no intention to continue my career in academia. I was nearing my mid-30s and was fairly accomplished in my position as a high school head in Bangkok, Thailand, and my resume, besides my doctoral thesis, had nothing much about being scholarly, which is research and publication. The offer to join as a visiting scholar at my alma mater upon completion of my PhD degree came as an accidental surprise. Upon persuasion and support from my supervisor and husband, I decided to enter academia and move to Malaysia at the end of 2013. I do sometimes wonder if, had I intended on joining academia after my doctorate, I would have planned my way more strategically. For example, engage more in research and publication and other scholarly activities and establish national and international connection with academics.

Nevertheless, despite a late start in academia, the journey remained meaningful where I grew as an educator and a researcher. When I joined academia, I was a fairly mature woman in my 30s with a well-formed identity as an individual and an educator. I saw educational research as an excellent tool for solving serious educational issues such as enhancing students' motivation and engagement, interests and attitudes towards learning, and reducing dropouts, anxiety and stress for learning. My beliefs in applied educational research on psychological constructs were steadfast. I believe research-based educational intervention can enhance teaching and learning strategies and improve students' behaviours and attitude towards learning. I was determined that my work will not sit on the bookshelves or in journal volumes; instead, it will bring impact and practical change to education in general and society at large. It is interesting how my utopian ideas were challenged later in my career, which I will discuss later in the sections below. Currently, I have nearly 8 years of experience in academia with experience of teaching educational psychology and psychology at both undergraduate and postgraduate levels in Malaysia and China. I have a number of research projects, more than 80 quality publications and international collaborators, over 400 citations in Google Scholar. I sit on the editorial board of a few reputed journals and have impressive grants and research supervision to my credit. In 2020, I was appointed as a fellow of the International Society for the Scholarship of Teaching and Learning (ISSOTL). In 2017, I was awarded by Scientific Publications Council of Ministry of Education, Malaysia, for a publication; in 2019, I was a recipient of excellent service award at University Utara Malaysia. I have coordinated several school levels committee in my previous university and currently I am the course coordinator for psychology at Wenzhou-Kean University. So, despite my relatively late start to academia, and not initially having the intention to follow an academic career, I have been able to follow a meaningful path and thrive in my academic roles.

INSTITUTIONAL CULTURES

Institutional culture has a central role in forming an academic's identity and setting the direction for an individuals' academic career. I started my academic career in Malaysia and was fortunate to become a part of a fairly huge, well-established state-funded public university that offered four-year bachelor's degrees, master's degrees and doctorate degrees in a wide range of social sciences and humanities disciplines. Under the implementation of the internationalisation policy of Malaysian Higher Education (MOHE, 2011), the university was set to hire a specific number of international academics identified as 'visiting lecturer'. That also meant the opportunity of working with other foreign scholars alongside the local scholars. Foreign academics, like me, were appointed on yearly or bi-yearly or sometimes longer contracts at all levels, such as assistant professors, associate professors and full professors based on their experiences and achievements.

The university operated under a number of national initiatives and schemes for advancing academic scholarship; however, I choose to highlight the initiatives that were directly concerned with foreign 'visiting' academics. The most prominent feature of this university culture was, which of course was guided by the national agenda, to keep up with the latest research, teaching and learning trends to stay at par with prominent higher education around the world. The university's Research and Innovation Centre (RIMC) intensely focussed on producing high-impact research outputs, which also meant achieving higher national and international ranking and national status of a research university. These aspirations translated into creating a conducive ecosystem for academics such as provision of international, national and university grants, training for research and publishing, establishment of high-quality journals (e.g., *Malaysian Journal*

of Teaching and Learning, MJLI) and innovation and creativity contests.

The university's Teaching and Learning Centre (UTLC)
and RIMC provided phenomenal support for those who
wished to excel in teaching and research. Most academics,
including myself, had moderate teaching assignments (nine
credit hours a term which translates into three courses to be
taught once a week for 3 hours each). I taught educational
psychology courses to diploma, undergraduate and postgraduate students and also had an opportunity to supervise
master and doctoral level research. There were numerous
opportunities for external (national) and university grants
with a generous amount of funding, sufficient to pursue large
social science investigations. Consequently, UTLC offered
innumerable professional development opportunities and
other relevant support for research and pedagogical
advancements for its faculty. Visiting international scholars
were encouraged to initiate and establish international collaborations by signing MoU (memorandum of understanding)
with universities abroad. These collaborations functioned
under department-level appointed committees. The university
also gave generous financial support for faculty (primary)
supervisors to facilitate doctoral research. This account more
or less explains the broad institutional and work culture for
my 7 years of academic work in my first institution.

GLOBAL ACADEMIA

I would like to use the term 'global' to discuss academia and
its associated expectations at the international level, which is
far and beyond one's institutional requirement. To be able to
connect with global academia and gain recognition, generally,

scholars engage in publishing in international journals, obtain international funding, membership or affiliation with international academic bodies, gain international recognition for research, academic development, publication or supervision, reviewing articles, serve on editorial board of international journals and work as thesis examiners for institutions outside of their country. In some cases, establishing a scholarship and academic credibility is significantly dependent upon obtaining recognition with global academia.

While all academics are expected to forge international connections, in my opinion, it is imperative for international academics to operate outside of the expectations laid by institutional policies. International standards for scholarship not only provide diverse ways of growing as scholar but also offer quality insights and exemplars to function at broader level as an academic. The implicit requirements set forth by global academia for establishing teaching, research and publication scholarship significantly shape the decisions and pathways for early career academics, should they choose to participate in it. Building an international network for research, publication, conferences and capacity-building collaborations is fundamental to establishing a solid academic profile.

SPACE FOR CONVERGENCE – CHALLENGES AND OPPORTUNITIES

Teaching and Learning

It is believed that academics operate in silos in their ivory towers, disassociated with the real-world issues, and little is known about the circumstances and varied spaces wherein they operate and how it shapes their trajectories as academics.

I chose to share my story from the three spaces that I described earlier and how the elements and expectations from each of these spaces have sometimes collided to induce conflict yet converged at some point to create a thriving space for an international academic like me.

My prior experience of working with K-12 education in a foreign culture facilitated in paving pathways for me to teach at the tertiary level in a new culture. In other words, my pedagogical experiences of teaching young students of other cultures immensely helped me in designing my andragogy efficiently. For example, it was easy for me to comprehend individual differences emanating from various sources (cognition, culture, language, etc.) and how they could influence learning progress, irrespective of learners' age. I also realised that adult learners equally enjoy hands-on and active learning as much as young learners. I was extremely pleased with the autonomy to design learning instruction and assessment at the tertiary level which allowed great flexibility in assisting learning. My professional background in education and my specialisation in educational psychology both proved extremely valuable in defining my teaching and learning practices in higher education. In the new role of teaching adult learners, I not only navigated this space with minimal challenges and surprises but also made this as a source of my several subsequent research topics. My teaching evaluations of all these years, the scholarship of teaching and learning (SoTL) award and research, active involvement and accomplishments of Students as Partners (SaP) pedagogical approach are evidence of my teaching excellence and meaningful student–teacher relatedness. A passion for teaching excellence can be a key for any academic. Acknowledging the fact that we are teachers first and disciplinary experts second reinforces academics will to accomplish teaching excellence. I highly recommend academics to actively engage in academic and professional development activities at their institutions and make teaching research part of their identity as an academic.

Research and Supervision – Mentoring and Collaborations

Unlike teaching and learning, research was challenging for me. Through my experiences of doctoral studies, I was under the impression that one can choose to pursue personal research interests and seek answers to all questions that intrigued them in their professional career. Little did I know about the need for alignment of one's research interest and expertise with their departmental needs and niche area, institutional focus and national agenda. For example, to obtain national funding, it is necessary to articulate how your research investigations will serve the national focus areas that communicate needs and priorities set by the government at the national level. Similarly, university-level funding required my research to be designed to accomplish the objectives set at the higher management level of the institutes. For example, the university student development centre may be interested in implementing a research-based soft skill development programme as per the need analysis survey of the university. It was a revelation that contradicted my utopian ideas for applied research and informed me that with conditional availability of funding and job requirement, it is not easy to pursue personal interest areas. Nevertheless, this requirement made sense to me; since we were using public money, it has to be put in the public interest. I learnt to align my personal research interests around the research needs of the funding agencies, which strengthened my enquiry approach providing a broader perspective. This strategy yielded fruitful results and I was able to secure grants.

Working on these research grants bought me a realisation that being an international academic, I was a part of academia; however, I was still an outsider in more than one way. The academic mobility policy under internationalisation thrust did not have the provision for foreign (visiting) academics to lead grants or funded projects at the university or national level. Thus, foreign academics could only participate in funded research as a member or proxy lead. This arrangement, in the beginning, dissuaded me to some degree in conceptualising personalised enquiries. However, very soon I realised that participating as a member with principal investigators in their research proposal, writing projects and pursuing the enquiry as a team can be an enlightening experience in developing my research skills. While recognition as a primary investigator is important, experiencing mentoring from senior and experienced researchers is critical for early career researchers to hone their research skills which not only includes conceptualising a research topic and methodology but also teamwork, communication and delivery on time. Nevertheless, this limitation later prompted me to focus my attention on teaching and learning in higher education. I could initiate and pursue this interest in my teaching contexts through action research and SoTL approaches with minimal financial support from the institutions and the funding agencies. I was able to lead self-initiated teaching and learning enquiries which lead to developing expertise in SoTL and I was able to secure ISSOTL fellowship.

The case for doctoral supervision practices was similar. International (visiting) scholars were not allowed to serve as the primary supervisors and could practice supervision only by becoming a second supervisor. This constraint limited me from choosing students with research topics that fell within my area of interest and expertise. I had to opt to work with other academics to assist their students' research in their interest areas. There might have been some justification for this policy unknown to the foreign scholars; nonetheless, becoming a co-supervisor in research supervision or member in research eventually turned out beneficial to me in several ways. Both research and supervision are two scholarly academic activities that are fairly high stake as the former involves financial and the latter moral obligation of supervising students in an appropriate and timely manner. Therefore, for an early academic, it is best to operate under mentorship which is fair and inclusive and creates enough opportunities for one to grow to accomplish initial assignments. I think, despite institutional policy-related limitations, I was fortunate to receive meaningful support, coaching and mentoring in both areas and was able to develop my research and supervision expertise. To date, my five doctoral students have successfully graduated and two are on-going, for which I served as a primary supervisor for one and secondary for the rest.

Along with those opportunities, it also provided me with a diversity of experiences of collaborations depending on the type of mentor I received. On most occasions I was invited by primary supervisors who were seniors and locals. I closely watched how they navigated through institutional formalities, interacted and built knowledge with students through agreement and disagreements and opened ways for students to learn. I gradually tried to understand their cultural values such as what could be offending and what is considered respectful.

Those experiences helped me decipher the meaning and intentions of such academic collaborations between senior academics and early career academics. It also made me concur with Macfarlane (2017) who calls academic collaborations beneficial in many ways but a problematic concept in some ways. According to him, academic collaboration occurs on the moral spectrum that ranges from 'intellectual generosity' and 'mentorship' to unfair practices such as 'cronyism' and 'parasitism' (pp. 476–478). It is highly likely that early career researchers recruited under academic mobility initiatives on open contracts with a complete absence of tenure track opportunities may easily succumb to the ills of the other end of that moral continuum. However, there are opportunities for early career researchers that I was fortunate to avail to receive meaningful mentorship which provided numerous opportunities for my career development.

I feel that the right kind of mentorship and later collaboration and association with individuals and organisations is central in determining academic career pathways for early career academics. To be able to avail quality mentorship, I feel it is an individual's imperative to systematically seek appropriate occasion and approach for appropriate support to initiate collaboration and/or association. This is where my connection with my global spaces turned out to be extremely valuable.

Institutional and Global Expectations – Widening Network and Growth

Institutional policies are significant in carving pathways for early career academics, be it local or international. For example, key performance indicators (KPIs) mentioned in one's job contract become annual goals to be accomplished for reappointment. This way, through institutional requirements, those KPIs are able to determine goalposts and shape academic progress for the academics. International academics, in my institutional context, given their status have rare opportunities to lead or provide university service which may prove deficit for their future career prospects; however, focussing on other KPIs can help fill this gap to an extent.

Among several KPIs, the requirement to publish in high-impact indexed journals was one that turned out to be extremely valuable in defining my career as a scholar. Publishing experience with some of the top journals in my area of research provided me an excellent training to think like a seasoned researcher, articulate arguments critically and utilise innovative and robust methodologies. Most prominently, with quality publication in indexed journals, my visibility began to increase at the national and international levels. For example, I frequently received invitations to review articles for some of the most prestigious journals in my field like *Assessment and Evaluation in Higher Education* or to become a thesis examiner from abroad (e.g., Deakin University, Australia) or was invited to provide talks. I was able to collaborate with researchers in Thailand, Indonesia, Saudi Arabia and New Zealand through publications.

The opportunities to expand academic career trajectories are numerous within and outside of the institution as well as international level. The first step to this is building meaningful networks at national and international levels for pursuing research and publication together. Join scholarly societies, attend and organise academic talks and workshops, share your scholarly activities at national and international platforms and engage in reviewing process.

I began with focussing on state-of-the-art academic development programme that the university offered throughout the year. The trainers were usually well-known experts from abroad who would train the local trainers to carry forward the training. Among several trainings, workshop series on the SoTL transformed into something very significant for me. My professional identity as an educator grounded in educational psychology research immediately provided me with a strong connection with that area. I accomplished a number of SoTL projects and published their outcomes in reputed journals in teaching and learning. This achievement established my credibility as an SoTL expert within my university and outside. I began to receive invitations to train novice SoTL practitioners in Malaysia. Eventually, as I became aware of the value of participating in global academia, I became a member of the ISSOTL, and in 2020, I received ISSOTL fellowship for demonstrating excellence and impact through my SoTL practices.

I also became a forerunner in establishing student-faculty partnership-based collaboration for teaching and learning in the Malaysian university I was working at. This practice helped me connect with the *International Journal of Students as Partners* (IJSaP) to become part of their editorial board. My work association with prominent scholars associated with the journal, which also translated to a variety of other academic collaborations, became extremely valuable to me as I learned immensely from their wisdom and practices. I now consciously seek connection with academics and scholars outside the institution. Many of them have mentored me with their rich experience and some of them have served as role models for me to emulate the path for success in academia. Currently, I am in China in a Sino-American university. It means I continue to forge new academic relationships at national and international level, discover teaching and learning with students from China and continue growing as an international academic.

CONCLUSION

Traditionally, most academics have followed the path with pre-set norms and requirements to accomplish their scholarly journey. While the path and goalposts continue to be more or less the same, the advent of internationalisation and academic mobility has altered the contexts and conditions for several academics like me. Cresswell (2014) states that 'mobility involves a fragile entanglement of physical movement, representations, and practices' and is 'a resource that is differentially accessed' (p. 21). It is difficult to say that the academic pathway for an international academic is either full of challenges or opportunities, but it's clear that the ability to tackle those challenges skilfully and optimise the opportunities provided with tenacity can ensure promising outcomes.

The quality of being foreign in terms of one's national, racial or religious identity in an international academic landscape and the 'otherness' often adds to the challenges of charting away in academia. The questions of power, knowers and knowledge contribute to the complexities of this journey. The nature of job contracts which do not promise tenure track or stability and are renewable based on several matrices that are directly related to the international academic, for example, performance, or indirectly related, for example, federal funding for the university, put such academics in a precarious position. Given the lack of opportunities to lead grants, or supervise thesis as primary supervisor, and the limited opportunities to lead or provide university service, it is important to forge ways to fill these gaps and thrive on the opportunities that are available for progression. Despite those limitations, I believe that my journey from my positionality and my given institutional culture and with the presence of global academia has so far been meaningful and accomplished.

To summarise, I would like to reiterate the need to optimise opportunities that come your way as an international career academic, among which seeking mentorship and collaboration of 'intellectual generosity' in and outside your institution are fundamental to your growth as an early career international academic. Essential skills like research, publication and supervision can be efficiently achieved by seeking mentoring and support from senior colleagues.

Second, it is important for international academics to operate and perform outside of institutional KPIs. The opportunities like high-impact publications, securing international grants in collaboration with experts in the field or international collaboration at any scale yield valuable results for personal and career growth.

Finally, opportunities to participate in academic development activity offered within and outside your institutions to build your professional profile are something never to be missed.

REFERENCES

Cresswell, T. (2014). Friction. In A. Petal (Ed.), *The Routledge handbook of mobilities* (pp. 107–115). London: Routledge.

Macfarlane, B. (2017). The paradox of collaboration: A moral continuum. *Higher Education Research and Development*, *36*(3), 472–485. doi:10.1080/07294360.2017.1288707

Ministry of Higher Education. (2011). *Internationalisation policy for higher education Malaysia*. Putrajaya.

7

AN INTERNATIONAL EARLY-CAREER ACADEMIC JOURNEY IN AUSTRALIA

Jasvir Kaur Nachatar Singh

ABSTRACT

Numerous studies have explored international students' and graduates' experiences around the globe but with less emphasis on exploring international academics' experiences. Internationalisation of higher education is not only about international students, it also includes mobility of academic staff members. Therefore, this chapter reflects on my ups and downs as well as many other opportunities that I gained in a privileged journey as an international early-career academic from Malaysia. The chapter starts with my personal experiences of how I identify myself as an international academic, the motivations to migrate, professional challenges that I face not only as an international academic but also as an early-career academic, the strategies that I adopted to overcome the challenges and how I self-created opportunities not only for myself but also for other colleagues – international

*academics and early-career academics. I will end the
chapter with significant successes that came my way.*

Keywords: International early-career academic;
challenges; opportunities; strategies; successes; Malaysia

A LITTLE BIT ABOUT ME...

To provide context to this chapter, I would like to provide a
succinct background about myself before readers dive into
deeper reading of this chapter. I was born in Malaysia and
completed my primary, secondary education and Bachelor's
degree in Malaysia. Since I was young, influenced by watching
Beverly Hills 90210 (now you can guess my age), I had always
wanted to study abroad, but I came from a humble background with my father as the only bread winner, mummy as a
housewife and three younger siblings. The only way to fulfil
my international dream was through securing scholarships.
Once I graduated with my bachelor's degree, I secured a
position as a professional staff member at a Malaysian university and then continuously applied for national and international scholarships to study abroad. I was fortunate to
receive a four-month FUJITSU scholarship to pursue my
Postgraduate Diploma in Management at the Japan-America
Institute of Management Science, Hawaii, and then we had a
week-long study tour in Japan. I had a great time in Hawaii
and Japan and made global friendships.

Upon completion, I returned to my job at the Malaysian
university and I applied for a Malaysian government scholarship to study for my master's degree and PhD in Australia. I

secured the scholarship and left to study my master's degree at Monash University, Australia. Upon my return for a short holiday, my funding for PhD studies was on hold due to the financial crisis. I then started my PhD in Malaysia for a year before applying for a prestigious Endeavour Postgraduate Scholarship from the Australian government. I was fortunate to receive the Endeavour scholarship and started my PhD at La Trobe University. While studying, I got married in Australia and hence remained in Australia to live and work. Upon graduation, I was employed on a contract as an Early Career Development Fellow (Associate Lecturer) at the Department of Management, La Trobe Business School. Within two years, I was offered a continuing position at the same department. I have recorded more fully my career journey in a book chapter (refer to Singh, 2020).

I consider myself an international academic as I was born and educated overseas. My research expertise is in the higher education discipline with a particular interest in exploring international students' current issues such as their academic success, lived experiences, employability and career aspirations, and learning experiences in a blended learning environment. In addition, I am also exploring international academics' leadership experiences, such as their challenges and opportunities in Australian higher education. Hence, this chapter reveals my ups and downs as an early-career international academic in the Australian higher education system.

DEEPEST DARKEST BARRIERS...

This is the first time I have openly revealed and written about the significant barriers that I encountered as an international academic working in an Australian university. I mean no disrespect to anyone or to the higher education institution that I am currently working in. But I do want to provide an account of authentic experiences that I have had and hopefully others will have much more pleasant academic journey as an early career international academic. I know it can be tough at times, but hang in there, you can – and will – make it. Now let me take you on a journey where I reveal my deepest darkest barriers as an early career international academic.

It started off when I was about to complete my PhD: my second supervisor passed away. I was extremely close to her. I did my master's thesis with her and she was one of the main reasons I came to La Trobe to do my PhD, as she had moved from Monash. I had wonderful supervisors. My primary supervisor is a gem of a person who supervised me until I graduated and we are still publishing together. But he left the university for another university just before I graduated. So that left me 'hanging' and striving on my own without any support from my supervisor, as well as grieving the loss of a close colleague and research mentor. Don't get me wrong, I had the best supervisors but it is just hard to be 'alone' in a setting with which I am unfamiliar with. Yes, I did have experience working as a casual teaching staff member and a research assistant at various Victorian universities, but it is not the same when you graduate and you are looking to advance or take the next big step in your career. I do not want to be hand-held, but I wanted someone to be there to guide and mentor me on what to do next.

I somehow landed a contract job as a Associate Lecturer at the department where I am based now seven months after my graduation. I am very grateful and thankful that within two years I was offered a full-time continuing lecturer position in the same department. This means a lot to me as I have somewhat secure job in an Australian university. Someone told me that you are so lucky to be on a continuing position as our job in the university is a precarious one. It did not resonate with me because in Malaysia, once you are in the system, you are never going to be thrown out. It is a very different scenario in Australia – and I am still grappling to understand this concept.

The biggest challenge I faced was how to navigate the academic work culture which I was definitely not accustomed to as yet. I was a 'newbie' in the department, without any 'tribe', mentors, supervisors or friends. I slowly found out that I needed a tribe or team to succeed, I needed a mentor to fast-track my career and I needed a supervisor who could help me thrive. I had none of these. I was all alone, by myself, always. I was told off by many Australian staff members, including superiors, who just thought I was inept, which really crushed my confidence as an international academic.

Another challenge I had was there was no one at my department who was interested in researching international students – which has been my research passion since I undertook my PhD exploring the notion of academic success of postgraduate international students and factors as well as challenges related to their academic success. This was a significant barrier to my research trajectory because I did not know anyone in my current institution who shared this passion. As an international academic, to form a significant network is crucial from the start because it will provide strong insights into the current research landscape in the institution as well as further abroad.

In terms of teaching, I did not face many challenges as I worked as a teaching associate for a number of years while doing my PhD. Therefore, I had some teaching experience in Australia prior to obtaining my contract employment. However, I had, and still have, some difficulties in managing students' expectations due to my culture, education and personal values. I received my undergraduate education in Malaysia and worked in one of the top Malaysian universities, so my view of a student-academic staff relationship is very different from that of my Australian colleagues, who treat students like friends and very empathetic towards students' needs. I had and still have some reservations about treating my students as friends due to the position of power that I have as a lecturer. This also means that I still have that concept embedded within me that students need to respect me as a lecturer due to my position. I am still learning to overcome this barrier. My latest research with my teaching associate is about exploring our teaching experiences as international academics during COVID-19 (Singh & Chowdhury, 2021).

SELF-CREATED OPPORTUNITIES...

In 2018, I attended one of many workshops at my current university, and I remember this scenario very well. One international academic who happened to be a professor talked of self-inviting himself to many conferences, workshops and other related opportunities because no one invited him in his early academic career days. There was a laughter in the room, but his concept of self-inviting really resonated with me. This is because, as an early-career international academic with limited networks and support, no one invited me to anything. I attended (and still do) numerous workshops organised by the university, and I hear all these wonderful stories of collaborations, invitations and so forth, but it did not happen to me.

Therefore, I took a chance and self-created opportunities for myself. For example, for some of my overseas talks, I created opportunities for myself via connecting with scholars or practitioners in my field via LinkedIn and then pitching my research findings and ideas and also offering myself to be involved as a panelist or presenter either in research or teaching workshops. Often, departments and institutions look for prospects for external engagement and would jump at opportunities for innovative research and/or teaching seminar where their own academics might benefit. They would then often invite me, and there you go, a self-created opportunity!

During the first year of my position, I saw an Expression of Interest (EOI) to join a prestige research team which oversaw significant funding and led a research theme/cluster in my university. I knew I did not fit the criteria but I still approached the team leader and he just said put your EOI in and we will see how it goes. I did and I was accepted as an observer – good enough for me as an early-career researcher who had limited research opportunities, so this was a golden opportunity! After my appointment, I attended almost all the meetings, tried understanding the mechanics and dynamics of writing a grant application, assessed high-level grant applications, provided my opinion, but most importantly observed other research leaders and professors providing their justifications as to why this grant application is supported or otherwise. I gained numerous insights from this opportunity. Sadly, the research theme/cluster was then dissolved just before COVID-19, but the lessons learned, especially on how to write winning grant applications and what assessors look for in an application, will be with me forever.

I have noticed lately that I have been provided with numerous international and institutional opportunities, partly because along the way of self-creating opportunities, I have grown my network. Truthfully, I am over the moon because it is tiring to self-create opportunities for yourself – it takes a lot of time and patience. Some of the examples include being invited to be a panelist on a career development panel at my institution and internationally invited to be one of the academic committee members for a Forum and Symposium as well as conducting a consultancy research, just to name a few.

Although it is tiring to self-create opportunities, as you need to be constantly proactive on social media, attend numerous workshops and network either passively or actively, I think it is worth it because it teaches you to be humble and build your confidence. It will also enhance your tolerance level of getting a 'NO' answer, and many people have said NO to me, but I will not stop self-creating opportunities to enhance my career. The worst thing that can happen is people saying NO, and I am OK with that because my tolerance level is high.

TOOLS, TECHNIQUES, STRATEGIES…

Since I have had barriers so early on as an international academic, I have personally adopted several strategies to survive and thrive in Australia. These tools or techniques or strategies are not exhaustive; they are based on my experiences navigating my own academic journey and have been contributing to my success till now. These practices might resonate with other international academics, so pick, choose, adopt and customise to suit your personality in navigating your academic career.

To understand the Australian academic and institutional culture, I have been a regular participant at my university's early-career research-intensive workshops since 2016. These workshops have really assisted me in positioning myself as an international academic in Australia. I learnt that there were several national funding schemes (such as the Australia Research Council), I came to understand research impact, engagement and partnerships and, most importantly, got to know academic and professional staff members in my institution who were able to assist me in my research. I found one of my first institutional collaborators (now friend and also an international academic) through these workshops. We were sitting at a table and introduced ourselves, not knowing we had similar research interests. We are very comfortable working with each other and now we are collaborating with another international partner in the United Kingdom.

Since I do not have a research mentor because I am yet to find the right person to work with in my research area, I then 'stalk' high-flying academics' profiles in my area – quietly. I am very good at seeing patterns, so I look into their profiles and see what they have been achieving and then reflect on what I have to do next. That is a secret tool that I use to pave my way and track my achievements against theirs. I am amazed at how many awards, grants, fellowships, publications and other related research achievements they receive and most of the time they inspire me rather than making me feel insecure. I find it therapeutic somehow, because at least I know I am on the right track if I follow in their footsteps, from a distance. Another technique that I use to 'stalk' high-profile academics is through assessing national grants. From there I get to see their grant applications and most importantly the way they craft the application is mind-blowing to me as an early-career international researcher.

I am also an active-passive academic on social media such as Twitter and LinkedIn. What I mean by active-passive is that I am not a regular academic who will post or comment on others' work. I met an academic who related to me that she feels intimidated by the regular updates and posts, but to me I use these outlets to gain up-to-date knowledge in my research area. These outlets have also helped me gain international networks and collaborators and to showcase my research through highlighting my invited talks and publications.

Being an international academic, I leverage upon my international networks. I started looking outwards (outside of my Department and University) as opposed to inwards. I started drawing my network map so that I remember people and their research interests as I am quite forgetful. In my map, I list down who have I collaborated with and have connections at the moment, internationally or outside of my department or institution. As I have mentioned, I worked and started my PhD studies at a university in Malaysia, so I took the opportunity to re-build my connections with the Malaysian National Higher Education Institute, which is at the forefront in researching on higher education-related issues, nationally and internationally. Someone told me that it is important not to burn any bridges, as you may someday or somehow need their assistance for your career trajectory. And that has exactly happened to me because I have been appointed as an Associate Research Fellow at the Malaysian National Higher Education Research Institute and gained research grants and publication opportunities.

SUCCESSES THAT CAME MY WAY

On a positive note, after all the endured barriers, self-created opportunities and strategies in place, I have achieved some awesome successes that came my way. I am sharing this not to intimidate anyone, but just to share my 'ongoing light at the end of the tunnel'. I am sharing my successes in terms of teaching, research and academic citizenship.

Teaching

As I mentioned earlier, I had some teaching experiences as a sessional before gaining my first contract employment. Along the way, I had a great teaching mentor who shared with me some secrets on how to be an effective teacher. I still have her guiding me now, even though she has retired. But there is another teaching mentor who I worked with while on contract and she taught me how to design excellent assessment rubrics and curriculums, engage students with practical examples and, most importantly, have fun in teaching. We are still working together, and she brings energy to our teaching-related discussions. They were the reasons that I received two teaching awards, La Trobe University Citation for Outstanding Contribution to Student Learning and College Pro Vice-Chancellor's Teaching Award, within two years of being on contract employment. In 2020, to the best of my knowledge, I am the only international academic at my faculty to receive international teaching recognition as a Fellow from Advance Higher Education, United Kingdom.

Research

In recognition of my research excellence, I have received several institutional and international awards. In 2018, I was awarded the Best Presenter Award at the Global Higher Education Forum, Malaysia. This international recognition led to a keynote invitation to the International Research Writing and Design online seminar organised by Galgotias University, India, in 2021. In 2019, I received the Editor's Choice Award from the Journal of International Students and in 2017 I won the Sandbox Award at the Early Career Researcher conference, Australia.

I have also built an international profile in the field of internationalisation of higher education, where I have led international and national research partnerships, publications and grants with colleagues in six regions (Australia, Malaysia, Scotland, Sri Lanka, the United Kingdom and the United States), across four continents.

As a dynamic researcher, I have received over AUD$100,000 in internal and international funding. I have published, in total, 36 publications, with 14 journal papers (more than 70% in Q1 and Q2 journals), 5 book chapters, 1 textbox, 1 report, 5 referred conference proceedings and 10 non-academic publications (all as first author). Three edited books are underway with two contracts signed.

Academic Citizenship

I make an outstanding contribution in service and engagement through formal and informal leadership roles, not only to the university but also internationally. In terms of academic citizenship excellence, in 2020, I received an Innovation Cultural Quality award from my faculty for my contributions in the Leaders in Lockdown programme initiated by my MBA director. I have recently been appointed as the Department Research Seminar Coordinator.

Internationally, I have been appointed as the Lead Coordinator for the Internationalization Cluster at the Malaysian National Higher Education Institute. I have also led significant engagement with more than 100 international and domestic student leaders and volunteers in Australia and Malaysia through the development and delivery of a first-of-its-kind leadership training workshop.

These successes did not come in an instant. There is no quick fix in academia as you need time to know your surroundings, especially for international academics as you are in an unknown territory. It took me good 5 years to network with other researchers and teaching staff members, find my way to be comfortable in the Australian academia space, build long-lasting bridges with my overseas collaborators, be strategic and be patient; I guess these are good virtues to have.

Time will unfold all the hard work that one has put in. Also, remember to have fun along the journey as there are no short cuts, at least in my case.

THE JOURNEY CONTINUES...

There is no conclusion in this chapter because my journey as an international academic will continue, at least for now. My raw, truthful narrative of my journey as an early-career international academic in this chapter might empower, inspire, resonate, relate and encourage other international academics to thrive in competitive academia. I consider myself a 'young' international academic and my academic journey has just begun in Australia, so stay tuned and do send me an email if you are wondering what my next moves are.

I had (and still have) my fair share of struggles, but I must say I am contented and happy with my ups and downs as I reflect on my experiences through this chapter. I guess we all have and will have different journeys in academia, but more importantly find your own comfort space, tribe and network, and do not be shy in seeking help and thrive.

REFERENCES

Singh, J. K. N. (2020). Why should I walk the same career development pathways as everyone else? In N. Tran, T. Pham, M. Tomlinson, K. Medica, & C. Thompson (Eds.), *Developing and utilizing employability capitals: Graduates' strategies across labour markets* (Vol. 1). New York, NY: Taylor & Francis Group.

Singh, J. K. N., & Chowdhury, H. (2021). Early-career international academics' learning and teaching experiences during COVID-19 in Australia: A collaborative autoethnography. *Journal of University Teaching and Learning Practice*, *18*(5), 1–17.

8

MOVING IN AND COMING HOME: INSIGHTS FROM TWO EARLY CAREER RESEARCHERS IN JAPAN

Shannon Mason and Yusuke Sakurai

ABSTRACT

Within a higher education system in Japan that is often regarded as insular, but which is increasingly striving to become more global in its outlook and makeup, we are classified as 'international researchers'. Shannon entered Japan as a foreign migrant who was raised and educated in Australia, while Yusuke returned to his home country after 12 years abroad. This chapter provides an account of our personal experiences as two early career researchers beginning our academic careers in Japan.

Keywords: Early career researcher; internationalisation; Japan; mobility; tenure

INTRODUCTION

Japan's higher education system is one that is well-established and enjoys an esteemed reputation as a world leader in research. In the year ending March 2021, Japan ranked fifth in the world in terms of research outputs, after the United States of America, China, Germany and the United Kingdom (Springer Nature, 2021). The Japanese government's annual financial commitment to research and development is currently US$170 billion, the third highest in number and second highest as a percentage of Gross Domestic Product (at 3.4%, after South Korea at 4.1%) (UNESCO Institute for Statistics, 2021). Nevertheless, for early career researchers (ECRs) looking to pursue an academic career, there are considerable challenges. There is limited funding for doctoral and postdoctoral research, impossibly high expectations (Yamada, 2019), and few opportunities for secure employment (Mallapaty, 2018). These challenges are likely heightened for women, who make up less than 15% of researchers in Japan, due to pervasive gender biases throughout the education system (Osumi, 2018). The irony is that both of these under-represented groups contribute more to scholarly outputs in Japan than their counterparts (Mallapaty, 2018; Osumi, 2018).

The international standing of Japan's universities in recent years has been on the decline. There are a number of factors that contribute to this, including the changing demography of the country with a continuing and drastic decline in the youth population, the long-term economic recession that has cut into funding for research and development and the lack of graduates' readiness to work in a globalised work environment (Yonezawa, 2020, p. 45). As opposed to other relatively well-resourced higher education systems, Japanese higher education institutions are highly insular. There is little global mobility of researchers (Yonezawa, Horta, & Osawa, 2016), who are traditionally recruited largely from doctoral programmes at the same institution (Horta, Sato, & Yonezawa, 2011). So, while countries around the world have been striving for decades to gain a competitive edge in a rapidly internationalising higher education sector, Japan is somewhat behind. Various government and institutional initiatives over the past decades have aimed to address this, with varying degrees of success (Yonezawa, 2011).

Whether a direct or indirect result of formal policy, there is a small but increasing number of 'international' researchers in Japan. This chapter is written collectively by two such researchers who are navigating the first years of our academic careers in universities in different parts of the country. We are classified as 'international researchers' within our current employment contexts, with Shannon being a foreign migrant raised and educated in Australia and Yusuke being a Japanese national who completed his postgraduate training abroad in two countries. We are both positioned within the social sciences, an underfunded area of research, and one that is often heavily aligned with a domestic rather than international agenda. While our contexts are very different, our paths crossed several years ago through mutual acquaintances, and since that time we have shared our stories of being ECRs in Japan. Here, we reflect on the commonalities and differences of our experiences. In the following sections, we walk readers through the various stages of our career progress, from our initial decision, through the application process, the road to tenure (track) and the daily challenges of the working environment. We reflect on how our position as international researchers has shaped our experiences, for better or worse, and in turn in our development as researchers, and integration into Japanese academic life.

ON CHOOSING JAPAN

Shannon: A Professional Stepping-Stone

As I started to progress in my doctoral degree in Australia, I started applying for positions in local universities, after making the decision to move from school teaching to higher education. Secure jobs in Australia are scarce, and competition high. It soon became clear that getting even a casual position in Australia would be difficult without having already completed my PhD, a long list of publications and successful grants. This situation led me to consider a move to Japan. This might seem like an unusual choice, but it was not purely a professional one. I had lived in Japan previously and have familial connections through my partner, so the language and culture were familiar to me. Because I had skills that I knew would be valued (teaching experience, English and Japanese language proficiency), I thought it would be an opportunity to get my foot in the door, to gain some experience and put me in a stronger position for future opportunities, wherever they may be.

Yusuke: On Returning to Japan

My job seeking experiences could be likened to a long and bumpy road. Towards the end of my PhD in Finland, I applied for about 15 posts and postdoctoral fundings in Japan and Finland. Thankfully, I had a reasonable 'Plan B'; my supervisor suggested that I go to Chile where she had a collaboration project to do postdoctoral work. At the same time, however, I also considered my career trajectory after the postdoctoral phase. I was 35 then, and if I would have taken the five-year position in Chile, my next job seeking round would come again in five years when I would be around 40. I felt that it would be unlikely for me to get a job since academic rank is closely linked with ones' age in Japan. So, it would likely be too late to enter the Japanese academia at a commensurate rank, and therefore I chose to come back home to Japan at that time.

Reflections

For many globally-mobile researchers, Japan may not immediately come to mind as a place to begin an academic career. For us, familiarity with the higher education system and the broader culture of Japan was perhaps just as important as the 'global capital' that appears to be sought after by universities in Japan. Indeed, many Japanese institutions are looking to diversify their researcher workforce, and as a result, opportunities are increasingly becoming available explicitly for international researchers. With this decision made, the next hurdle was to start on the application treadmill.

ON THE APPLICATION PROCESS

Shannon: Faxes, Photocopies and Applications for Foreigners

I can't remember how many jobs I applied for, I think it was more than 20, and they each involved filling in very specific information in a very specific way, as well as a lot of photocopying to make multiple packs of documents for each member of the selection committee, all of which had to be sent by registered international mail (with queries answered by fax!). From memory, there was not a single online application. While I applied for all jobs that I felt I would be competent to take on, I did concentrate on those applications that were specifically looking for international faculty. Indeed, all the call-backs I received (about five) and the interviews I completed (two) were for short-term contract positions specifically for foreign faculty and involved English-teaching duties.

Yusuke: Don't Think, Just Accept

The road was long and bumpy, and eventually after a year my efforts resulted in securing a fixed-term contract. At a local conference, a professor at a large Japanese university approached me about a new post that would open soon and asked to hear about my major teaching areas. I submitted a series of documents, hoping for a positive result. However, it was not successful, and I got a private message from the professor explaining that the major reason that the other committee members were not happy with my application was that I had limited teaching experience in Japan, although I had more than ten years of experience abroad. I felt disappointed that my overseas experience was not fairly evaluated in Japan. My stressful job application processes continued for about four years. I ended up with 31 unsuccessful applications until I got an offer for my current tenure-track post. I still dream how many articles I could have written if the process had been much smoother.

In addition, I often felt uneasy about the fact that most interview committees, usually composed of about five interviewers, were heavily male-dominated. I have been invited to six or seven interviews in Japan and saw only five women committee members in total. In contrast, more than half of committee members in a Finnish university interview were women. I do not know if there were any concrete impacts on my applications, but it just felt awkward, although not surprising when you consider the gender balance in the Japanese academe.

Reflections

As we noted earlier, both the Japanese government and individual institutions are looking to increase the international outlook of their higher education workforce. The application process, however, does not appear to be conducive to the recruitment of applicants outside of the country. It is very interesting to note that for Shannon, while international experience was considered an asset, for the most part it related to English language skills. For Yusuke, his many years of international experience does not seem to have been valued to the extent that it might be expected, considering the constant focus on internationalisation. It may be that the potential added value is not obvious despite the potential 'ripple effect', bringing in new insights, different worldviews and promising connections to benefit the institution more widely. While there are positions that are made specifically to meet international agenda, there may be a focus on language instruction or, at best, English medium instruction rather than the various disciplines and scholarly activities in which international researchers engage.

ON GETTING TENURE (TRACK)

Shannon: It's Who You Know, and Lucky Timing

There was no possibility of tenure at my first job in Japan; that was made explicitly clear. I became very aware of the need to get a permanent position as soon as possible considering my age, as Yusuke noted earlier. I had started teaching a course as a casual tutor at a nearby university, as is common practice, and over a few years got to know the staff and students. When a tenured position came up I applied, and in the interview all of the selection committee members knew (of) me, and this was undoubtedly vital in the successful outcome. My PhD was complete by this point, and I had a healthy list of publications. However, it was very clear to me that my teaching experience (as might be expected in a faculty of education) and my ability to engage in the Japanese work environment were valued much more than my international status. Further, being both a young researcher (under 40) and a woman also played in my favour as these groups are both under-represented in Japanese academia.

Yusuke: It's Who You Know, Yes! but a Miracle May Occur

Pursuing a PhD abroad, I had a weak social network with Japanese researchers. I knew this would be a problem if I wished to secure a position in Japan, so I participated in some Japanese conferences while I was still undertaking a PhD in Finland. The position I was ultimately successful in securing was a tenure-track position at a university where I knew no one, although I still do not know how my international experiences were evaluated. A part of the interview was conducted in English so this suggests this was a valued skill at least. As with Shannon, there were other factors that may have helped, such as the recent implementation of a government policy which directs Japanese universities to decrease the average age of their faculty communities. In 2019, the average age hit a record high at 49.4. The government has incentivised universities to increase the ratio of faculty members aged under 40 to greater than 30% (23.5% in 2016). This move was crucial for me since I was already 39 when I had an interview for my current post. I managed to get my foot in the quickly closing door.

Reflections

Having both come from higher education systems outside of Japan, it was not until we were in Japan that we were able to make stronger connections with the local research community, and to gain experience in local institutions, the latter appearing to be vital to gaining secure employment. While other characteristics also arguably placed us in a stronger position to gain tenure (such as our relatively young age which aligns with Japan's target of decreasing the average age of researchers), interest from employers focused more on our teaching experience and our proven ability to engage in the domestic academic environment, more than any skills or experiences that may contribute to the internationalisation of the institution, such as English-language publications, delivering courses in English, or engaging in international research collaborations.

ON EXPECTATIONS AND RESPONSIBILITIES

Shannon: Teaching, Teaching, Teaching (and Research in between)

There is an often unwritten rule of workload responsibilities afforded to scholars in Japan, that of one-third teaching, one-third research and one-third service. However, compared to colleagues in other parts of the world, I have a relatively heavy teaching schedule. I am responsible for 16 courses per year spread over two semesters of 15 weeks (one 90-minute class per week). As an English speaker, I have an explicit role in delivering courses in English, as well as several 'general English language' classes outside of my own faculty. This means that most of my research is conducted in small drips during semesters, with most progress being made in the periods between semesters, although during these periods there is often considerable time taken up with administrative work, particularly preparing and proctoring university entrance examinations and interviews. While research activities, outputs and grants are considered in annual performance reviews, I do not particularly feel the pressure to publish that I hear from colleagues in Australia. While I have strived to be productive in my research activities, this is more related to a desire to remain competitive in the international job market. However, research productivity is strained at times due to limited access to international literature databases and the lack of an ethics review board. This has resulted in me taking up an unpaid adjunct position in Australia, so that I can take advantage of these vital resources.

Yusuke: No One Talks about Research around Me

At my previous workplace, the director and colleagues were leading the overall internationalisation of the university and were considerate of their juniors' international activities. However, few people care about my English research outputs in my current position. I have some research financial support from the university but collegial support is non-existent and no opportunities for scholarly dialogues. There are no incentives, no supportive policies and there is no acknowledgement. Co-authored papers are less valued due to a prevalent belief that they are produced with less effort. Access to journal databases and software is limited, and so I have to pay for these with my own external grants. In addition, there is an untold expectation – sometimes explicitly expressed – that outputs should be in Japanese. Since I often collaborate with international researchers who do not publish in Japanese, I would need to set up another project solely for my Japanese language output. I believe that I will not write many Japanese articles in the future but instead I will write short 'reports' in Japanese for some websites and conference proceedings. Like Shannon related earlier, my motivation in sending out my outputs to an international arena stems from my intrinsic motivation to keep myself afloat with overseas colleagues.

In regards to teaching, a university leader explicitly said that young researchers are expected to concentrate more on teaching than on research. I have six different courses per semester including undergraduate and master's courses which take up most of my time. Furthermore, there are long meetings, advising local school teachers, post/undergraduate students' thesis reporting days, interim thesis reporting days, open campus events and entrance examinations. Through these commitments, of course, I have learned better how the institution works. However, if I had a reasonable balance between research, teaching and service responsibilities, I would probably see my teaching and service responsibilities in a more positive light. I am not sure whether my re-entry to Japan was a good choice since I feel that my academic experiences and skills have not necessarily been positively recognised.

Reflections

While scholars in Japan are expected to engage equally in teaching, research and service, in both of our cases there is a strong emphasis on teaching, which may be felt more strongly for us being in the social sciences. In any case, the heavy teaching and administrative workload leaves little time for research. While we may not feel the same intense pressure to publish as our colleagues in other countries, we also do not have access to the resources and support that our international colleagues may have. This not only provides a barrier to our individual research productivity but also to the internationalisation agenda of institutions, by not harnessing the skills that international researchers bring.

ON WORK-LIFE BALANCE

Shannon: A Good Balance Not Possible for All

One of the educational issues that I have researched is teacher workload, and so I am very aware that Japan is notorious for its long working hours. Working long hours is often seen as a badge of honour, although attitudes are changing, but as a foreign researcher I tend not to be strongly influenced by this social expectation. This may only be possible because of the context in which I work, being in a social sciences faculty working in an individual office, as opposed to working in a lab with multiple researchers of various rank and the social norms that go with that, for example, the expectation that younger researchers do not leave before their 'superiors'. I also work in a national university, and so laws and regulations are strictly adhered to. For example, if I am required to work on a weekend on occasion, I am given a day off in lieu, and administration will chase me up to make sure that I take it. For the most part, I feel that I have a good work-life balance, which is not something I ever would have thought possible in Japan (and talking to colleagues in Australia is something they struggle with greatly). Nevertheless, it is a constant and conscious choice to judiciously accept projects, invitations and requests in order to maintain that balance.

Yusuke: A Japanese Should Be like Japanese?

Work-life balance is also a tricky part of working in Japan. I learned how researchers outside of Japan worked, and it was different from that in Japan. Important decisions are made over emails during weekends and even at night. I have stopped responding to emails after around 6 p.m. and weekends. If you respond to them, email interaction continues forever and even into the night. I believe that Japanese academia needs more people who hold different understandings about work, personal life and the balance between them. In this regard, it needs a critical mass of a diverse faculty cohort which includes those who look different and indeed work differently in Japan. I look like a typical Japanese, so I feel the pressure to be 'Japanese'.

Reflections

Gaining a personally satisfying work-life balance is a challenge for academics in all parts of the world, and while Japan is notorious for long working hours, the extent to which a work-life balance is possible may be dependent on various contextual factors. Recent work regulations and laws may protect academics, and changing views about work may serve to protect them, but the practices and attitudes of colleagues can mitigate these opportunities. It may require making and enforcing personal decisions regarding drawing a line between professional and personal life. While this is likely necessary in any context, in Japan this can potentially be very challenging due to social norms and pressures.

BELONGING AS AN 'OUTSIDER'

Shannon: An Outsider to an inside Outsider

I have worked at two universities in Japan, and my position in both was quite different. In my first position, a short-term contract for an English language instructor, I was definitely separate from the rest of the staff and sometimes in quite obvious ways. For example, our stamp sheet where we sign in each day was in a different book than the Japanese staff, and we were not required to attend meetings. Wanting to be seen as a member of staff I began attending meetings in any case, and the following year had classes timetabled during that time so that I could not attend (this may have been, but was probably not, a coincidence). In my current university I am a member of staff, and although I am obviously an outsider, being the only permanent faculty member not born in Japan, I have the same expectations and responsibilities as anyone at my rank in the university. I know that this is not the case for all international researchers in Japan who may express a lack of belonging, inclusion and status. While I do feel that I am a valued member of my faculty, I am also strongly supported by researchers across the world who provide a sense of belonging to my wider disciplinary network. Perhaps if this network were not so strong, I may have a different perspective of my position in Japanese academia.

Yusuke: Seeking Membership at Home and across the Globe

To me, networking is problematic. As I noted earlier, I occasionally attended domestic Japanese conferences during my doctoral studies. When there were visitors from Japan in Finland, I hosted their visits. However, they were not necessarily interested in developing a network with me during their visits; they had their own aims. As such, it was not realistic to build on these opportunities. I think this situation affects my job applications (the more people you know, the more likely you are to get a job), access to new opportunities (collaborations and funding) and the impacts of my research (invited speakers and potential readers of my work). Nonetheless, the situation appears to be gradually getting better, but I need to continue my strategic effort to expand my network further. Simultaneously, like Shannon, I also attempt to continue my international connections. I have strived for some visibility at international conferences and online via social networking tools.

Reflections

In both of our cases it seems that our position as international researchers may place some limits to the extent that we feel a sense of belonging, and that appears to be dependent on the institutional environment. This environment may or may not promote collaboration with the increasing number of international researchers in Japan. For us, we seem to be not so focused on being a fully accepted and integrated member of a particular faculty or institution, but rather with the wider disciplinary community, both more widely within Japan and internationally. Without this focus we would not have met each other, being in different parts of the country and having different areas of research interest (although we have since realised many of our interests intersect). Thus, continuing to build our international networks (particularly online) is an important part of our sense of becoming an academic, regardless of our geographic location.

CONCLUSION

In this chapter we have reflected on our becoming and being international researchers in the social sciences in Japan. In sharing and reflecting on our own personal experiences, we hope we have provided some insights that may be of interest to other international researchers and particularly those who are looking to Japan as a potential country to begin an academic career. We must stress that the experiences of any researcher are highly personal and contextual and dependent on myriad factors, and so our stories are not typical, there is indeed no typical experience. However, in identifying some commonalities between our experiences, we would suggest that increasing one's chance of success in gaining and sustaining a fulfilling academic career in Japan may include: a knowledge of the norms of Japanese academia and the broader culture, building a network and personal profile within the country, promoting skills and knowledge that would benefit an internationalising sector, being aware of institutional regulations and legal rights regarding employment and expectations, and maintaining a strong support network with researchers in all parts of the world. Japan is in a state of flux as it adapts to its changing demography and the internationalising higher education sector. As with any system, there will be potential opportunities and challenges, and we hope our experiences have been of interest.

REFERENCES

Horta, H., Sato, M., & Yonezawa, A. (2011). Academic inbreeding: Exploring its characteristics and rationale in Japanese universities using a qualitative perspective. *Asia*

Pacific Education Review, 12(1), 35–44. doi:10.1007/
s12564-010-9126-9

Mallapaty, S. (2018). Short-term generation. *Nature Index,
555.* Article 67.

Osumi, N. (2018). Calling *rikejo*: A push for more Japanese
women of science. *Nature Index, 555.* Article 59. doi:10.
1038/d41586-018-02906-1

Springer Nature. (2021). Country/territory outputs. Retrieved
from https://www.natureindex.com/country-outputs/
generate/All/global/All/n_article

UNESCO Institute for Statistics. (2021). How much does your
country invest in R&D. Retrieved from http://uis.unesco.
org/apps/visualisations/research-and-development-spending/

Yamada, Y. (2019). Publish but perish regardless in Japan.
Nature Human Behaviour, 3, 1035. doi:10.1038/s41562-
019-0729-9

Yonezawa, A. (2011). The internationalization of Japanese
higher education: Policy debates and realities. In S.
Marginson, S. Kaur, & E. Sawir (Eds.), *Higher education
in the Asia-Pacific. Higher education dynamics* (Vol. 36).
Springer. doi:10.1007/978-94-007-1500-4_17

Yonezawa, A. (2020). Challenges of the Japanese higher
education amidst population decline and globalization.
Globalisation, Societies and Education, 18(1), 43–52. doi:
10.1080/14767724.2019.1690085

Yonezawa, A., Horta, H., & Osawa, A. (2016). Mobility,
formation and development of the academic profession in
science, technology, engineering and mathematics in East
and South East Asia. *Comparative Education, 52*(1),
44–61. doi:10.1080/03050068.2015.1125617

Section 3

PERSONAL AND FAMILY EXPERIENCES IN LONG- AND SHORT-TERM MOBILITIES

9

INTERNATIONAL ACADEMIC EXPERIENCES IN JAPAN

Ariunaa Enkhtur and Sainbayar Gundsambuu

ABSTRACT

The Japanese government has introduced various policies to attract highly skilled professionals including foreign faculties at higher education institutions. However, there is little guidance for foreigners, especially from the Global South to navigate the job hunting process. When we came to Japan to pursue our doctoral studies (along with a 7-year-old and a 7-month-old), we did not plan to work here afterward. However, learning the language (even at survival level), finding a mentor (inside and outside the university), actively participating in academic conferences, and being the agent in our study and work helped us overcome the roadblocks.

In this chapter, a husband and wife reflect on their academic journey abroad – challenges and opportunities – in Japan. We hope that our experience and advice would be useful for young families interested in pursuing education abroad and perhaps working in Japanese academia.

Keywords: Academic mobility; internationalisation of higher education; Japan; personal experiences; early career academics; family

INTRODUCTION

I was born and grew up in Ulaanbaatar, the capital city of Mongolia, and my husband (Sainbayar, whom we call Sainaa) was born and grew up in Tosontsengel, a rural town in Western Mongolia. Landlocked between Russia and China, Mongolia has vast land with only 3.2 million population and a very volatile, cold and dry climate – a complete opposite to Japan's landscape (surrounded by sea) and climate (warm and humid). Sainaa and I both graduated from Mongolian universities – both with English language major but from different universities. We got married shortly after starting our professional works in Mongolia. I worked in an educational non-government organisation (NGO) running study abroad projects while Sainaa taught English and translation studies at a national university in Mongolia.

I came from an academic family in Mongolia – both of my parents worked in academia their whole life. Although academic profession's pay rank is not high in Mongolia (thus, many promising graduates do not pursue academic jobs but rather prefer corporate employment), I grew up to love the nature of this profession – to learn, explore, share, and receive respect and dignity in return. So even though I chose a quasi-international organisation over university employment in Mongolia, I always had an aspiration to complete a PhD and work in academia. Sainaa is a first-generation student to go to college. As the eldest son in his family, he has always been a role model for his siblings. Therefore, since choosing a faculty job in a local university in Mongolia, Sainaa was aspired to excel in his job. However, without a PhD degree, he could not actively participate in academic committees or hold any leadership positions. Although he did not initially plan to do graduate schools abroad, he realised that education in the Global North had more to offer for his professional development in academia.

We began our academic journey abroad when we first set feet to America as Fulbright scholars (different programs in different states). I brought our 3-year-old son with me and Sainaa was 1,100 km away. It was an extremely challenging yet a growing process for me to navigate a graduate school and enrol my son in the pre-school system in the United States. Upon graduating, we returned to our old jobs and tried to apply what we learned in the United States. However, we still needed PhDs to build our careers in academia. So, after two years, we decided to pursue our PhDs in Japan – and the Japanese government scholarship made it happen.

As we look back on our academic journey for the last 10 years, we feel incredibly grateful for all the support we received on the way – in the United States, Mongolia and Japan from complete strangers to professors – that made it possible to complete our graduate schools in the United States and Japan and start our academic jobs in Japan. Our initial experience of living apart in the United States taught us the importance of seeking support beyond family members when necessary and the ways to handle emotional challenges.

Studying abroad with young children can be extremely challenging in many aspects – economically, socially, mentally and even physically. When we first came to Japan, we were accompanied by our then 7-year- and 7-month-old kids, and none of us had Japanese skills beyond 'hello' and 'thank you'. We spent the first few months in a crisis-like situation – trying to find baby food in the supermarket, learning the language from *Hiragana* – Japanese alphabet, preparing for graduate school exams while hunting for apartment and nursery school, preparing public school paperwork and the list goes on and on. Despite all the difficulties, studying abroad with your family can keep you focused and motivated to complete your PhDs, if there is support. Our professors were supportive of studying with young kids and understanding of our familial obligations. At the same time, they did not expect less from us for having young children. This high expectation gave us the confidence that we are able to complete our doctoral programs together.

In Japan, we were both in graduate school – together. I was on a government scholarship, and Sainaa was self-supported but received a full tuition waiver from the university. He could not compete for the government scholarship due to age restrictions. This meant we had to work while studying. In Japan, we could work outside the university – unlike in the US. To support our family, we worked both on and off campus – mostly teaching English in local schools and doing Teaching or Research Assistant jobs at our university. These casual jobs helped us secure academic jobs in Japan.

Another good point was that Japan has a very well-structured social support system – good national health care that is almost free for young children, a nursery school system and reliable public schools. Although nursery schools can have a long waiting list and can be difficult to enter depending on the city and district, luckily, as full-time students we were able to send our son to a nursery school. It was huge support for our family and helped us focus on our research.

We also shared similar research interests in education and studied under the same professor (although the committee members were different). I enrolled one year ahead, so my research was one year ahead of Sainaa's. This helped us understand one another's perspectives and enabled us to support each other emotionally and academically. We read each other's papers, discussed with each other and took turns in our research trips outside Japan or conference presentations so one of us can look after the kids. Because we were not in the same year, our schedules were also different, helping us avoid the same deadlines. There were many moments of frustrations, feeling stressed and overloaded with pressures – but we encouraged each other and reminded us that doing a PhD is not a straight A to B process but rather a very fluid process going around the same thing repeatedly. Even if we did not know yet where our research was taking us, we kept taking small steps – writing every day, completing small parts of the project – because we had no time and money to waste.

Some tips that helped us finish our programs in Japan include:

- *Seeing the PhD program as a project that must be completed in three years.* We planned major expected outcomes – journal articles, presentations in 3 years and set our goals accordingly. Then for each year, we had sub-goals to complete in the semester. Not everything went as we planned. In fact, we adjusted most of our plans. Nevertheless, it helped us see the big picture and how small pieces fit together.

- *Building a professional network in your research/discipline area.* Most associations have small subgroups by fields and interests of the members. If there is any professional network where graduate students, faculties and practitioners share practices, it is a good idea to join them.

My colleague who completed a similar program earlier than us, suggested to participate in networking sessions. She had introduced us to several groups early on, which was a tremendous help to build our research.

- *Having multiple mentors.* In Japan, the supervisor is the main mentor who guides the students and provides all kinds of support, from finding apartments to publishing papers. However, this is changing as more diverse students join programs from different backgrounds with different personal situations. Although professors' guidance was important, we took the initiatives to shape our research in ways that were meaningful for us professionally. Our study was related to our home country, so we sought research support beyond our professor and committee members who did not know much about Mongolia. This included finding mentorship from diverse areas – professionals in Mongolia, professional networks outside Japan, and sojourners from Mongolia who shared similar passions. Some associations have mentorship events and workshops for graduate students where senior faculties provide guidance. We attended these workshops, such as the one provided by Comparative and International Education Society (CIES) and found them very useful to improve our works and establish networks.

- *Applying for research grants and projects.* Even if you do not receive grants, applying for research grants is important. The most prestigious and common research grant for PhD students is the the Japan Society for the Promotion of Science (JSPS) fellowship. Although we did not receive the grant, our experience of writing proposals helped us win other grants from our university (e.g., scholarship for overseas fieldwork or scholarship for overseas conference presentation) that enabled us to attend various international conferences and conduct our fieldwork overseas.

- *Learn Japanese.* If you have family and would like to have a comfortable life in Japan, it is best to learn Japanese before coming to Japan. The Mongolian language has many similarities with Japanese in terms of grammar and sentence structure; however, it was still challenging to learn a new language while conducting research.

By the time I graduated, Sainaa was in his last year of the PhD program. So, I had to find a job to support my family, while waiting for Sainaa to complete his doctorate. I had been working for a year as a Research Assistant, and my professors proposed me to continue as a part-time researcher. In addition, I also had the opportunity to teach a class in the international undergraduate program at my university. Sainaa was also working part-time but was focused more on his thesis. Upon Sainaa's graduation, our eldest son completed his primary school and moved on to secondary school – asking us to stay in Japan a little longer as he did not want to be separated from his friends. Luckily, we both received work offers by then. I was offered to work as an assistant professor in my university's international division. Sainaa received job offers from a couple of other universities to teach English. Our jobs were highly relevant to our research interests and matched our aspirations. At the same time, we also had the opportunity to build professional networks in Japan and learn from Japan's higher education teaching and administrative practices.

WORKING AS EARLY CAREER ACADEMICS IN JAPAN
Job Hunting

Japanese higher education institutions are very diverse compromising of junior colleges, universities and graduate schools. Enrollment is also very high with over 80% of

18-year-olds in higher education (MEXT, 2017). Majority of universities are private (80%), and many are mainly teaching institutions. Therefore, there are generally more positions for teaching on part-time contract (adjunct contract). The data from 2016 show that 13,336 out of 22,329 faculties (60%) in Japan were part-time. In addition, most English native speakers work as English teachers in wide range of higher education institutions (HEIs) while faculties with proficient Japanese particularly those from China and South Korea are in STEM fields (Huang, 2018). For someone with little Japanese skills, non-native speaker of English, with PhD in social sciences and education, there are not many options. However, by the time we graduated, we realised that working in Japanese HEIs are becoming more welcome than we expected because we received a couple of offers.

With a rapid aging and low birth rate (a third of its population is predicted to be 65 and older by 2050), Japan has modified its immigration policies to attract highly skilled professionals and other skilled workers. In 2012, the immigration services introduced a point-based system for highly skilled professionals to give them preferential immigration treatment (The Government of Japan, 2017). The system enables a faster route to permanent residence. While other foreign workers become eligible to apply for permanent residence after 10 years of consistent work in Japan, those with highly skilled professional visas can apply after only 1–3 years. In addition, there are other preferential treatments such as allowing the spouse of the visa holder to work full time without a separate work visa.

In Japan, where universities have been mainly focused on educating the 18-year-old population, the low birth rate meant shrinking university students. As the traditional student population is shrinking, universities are more pressured to diversify their programs and enroll non-traditional students. Faculties with foreign background and education have much to offer in creating such programs approaching from different perspectives and tapping into their international connections.

Although many job calls are posted in online academic job search platforms (such as https://jrecin.jst.go.jp, managed by the Japan Science and Technology), each institution's requirements and application documents are unique – thus, taking enormous time and effort to prepare application materials. While research-oriented universities place more emphasis on research background and potentials for producing research outputs; teaching universities look at teaching certificates and past teaching experiences in Japan or overseas.

The most common start point in academia is to work as an assistant professor or lecturer with a fixed-term contract for a predetermined number of years, often up to 10 years (Green, 2019). Such jobs often carry the title 'specially appointed' – as is my title, 'specially appointed assistant professor'. It is generally difficult to get tenure track position at national universities. Therefore, during this 10-year-period, foreign faculties need to be very strategic in building their career. In many cases, they go to private universities for a tenured position where the tenure system can be more flexible.

When I was graduating from my PhD program, I found the job search process very confusing. The university provided a handbook for all foreign graduating students explaining Japan's job hunting process a year before we graduated. The book was in Japanese and it explained the job hunting process to be very formal – starting from a certain period only (around September), having a specific type of professional photo, dressed in a certain type of black suit (even the handbags need to be in a certain shape when the job applicant goes for an interview). The applicants had to prepare their application documents in handwritten using the employer's designated template. So, to help the international students navigate this complicated job-hunting process, our university offered trainings for international students. However, I learned that these training and job-hunting rituals mostly applied to those seeking company employment, not academic jobs. Confused with these rituals, we had not applied anywhere. However, our professor and peer students introduced us to our job positions and we were able to get these jobs after a rather less complicated application and interview process.

Research Experience (Ariunaa)

Most faculty positions in research institutions come with research funding; however, depending on the position some do not. As a full-time faculty, I was expected to contribute to research, teaching, society and administration equally. However, my temporary job post did not come with a research funding. Therefore, I had to apply for external competitive grants to conduct my research. The most common competitive grant for early career faculties in Japan is the Early Career Scientist grant from the Japan Society for the Promotion of Science (JSPS). JSPS has multiple grants and fellowships for scientists inside and outside Japan. Receiving this grant makes it possible for researchers to pursue their research independently and increases their research profile.

The grant-in-aid for early career scientists by JSPS is for individual researchers who completed their PhD in the last eight years to apply for up to 5 million JPY funding for 2–5 years. During the eight years since PhD, early career researchers can receive this grant up to 2 times. Compared to other JSPS grants, this grant has a very high acceptance rate at 30–40%. Since universities also benefit from the grants – in reputation, research outputs and administrative funding – they encourage faculties to secure outside competitive grants. Encouraged by the university, other professors, and peers, I prepared the application and applied for the grant. After 6 months of selection process, I secured a small grant, two million yen (about 17,000 USD) for three years. Having my own research fund has been very useful – I could hire a Research Assistant to help organizing my data, literature review and data analysis. In addition, my university offers research support for parents with small children – I also applied for this grant and was able to secure about 200 hours of research assistant's work. I dedicated this grant to another project to expand my research on Mongolian student mobility.

Sainaa, on the other hand, was not required to pursue research. However, he expanded his PhD dissertation and was able to submit two journal articles within 1–2 years. Although his job did not have a research component, he stayed on track and actively took part in research dialogues in his field – participating and presenting in conferences. As international conferences shifted towards online mode, he did not have to travel anywhere to attend these conferences.

Administrative and Teaching Duties

As Japanese universities are striving to become more international, there are more jobs that do not require proficient Japanese skills. Both of our jobs did not require proficient Japanese as we could work in English. However, it has been challenging for me to navigate faculty meetings and new faculty trainings that are often conducted in Japanese. In addition, administrative work moved faster when I communicated in Japanese – with support from colleagues. I found translation software, such as DeepL, handy – I always use it to prepare Japanese versions of various documents that I produce, to save time.

For Sainaa, his job has been mainly teaching – thus, relatively independent. Due to the nature of his job, teaching English, he worked with international teachers from different cultures who are all fluent in English. For his job, he needed to learn the new system of the universities, design his courses, attend few professional training workshops and teach academic courses in English. Due to the Covid-19 pandemic, he mostly taught from home, communicating only with students with little interaction with staff and other faculties. Ironically, although it saved him much commute time, about a round trip of three to four hours a day, he could not build much professional network or as much as he hoped for within that one year. However, he learned much about teaching methodologies from his peer faculties and from teaching Japanese students.

I also teach a course at my university, in a different department. Compared to Sainaa (who has over 15 years of teaching experience in Mongolia), my teaching experience is only limited to few classes I taught in Japan. While Sainaa went through a rigorous teacher preparation program in Mongolia, designed for all faculties, I did not receive formal training to teach students. Therefore, I still struggle to engage my students, particularly since it moved to online mode in 2020 due to the pandemic.

Japanese universities do not require faculties to have a teaching certificate; faculties with PhD degree are assumed to be experts in their fields, thus qualified to teach. Therefore, to help faculties build their teaching skills and other course management skills (along with other topics from research to management), my university offers various professional development workshops. As a new faculty member, I have to collect 30 credits in two years, but the topic can be anything from a workshop on designing a curriculum to a research publication workshop. However, most trainings are conducted in Japanese, putting those with low Japanese skills at a disadvantage. On the other hand, trainings specific to natural sciences and engineering are in English. This has been very challenging for me to fully take advantage of these trainings. According to Huang's research (2018), most foreign faculties in Social Sciences and Humanities fields, except those teaching English and English-taught programs, have proficient Japanese skills. Although this case is changing as universities hire more faculties with low Japanese skills, it will probably take some time to make trainings more accessible.

Mentorship

It is very challenging for foreign professionals just starting a professional career in Japan to navigate their work system without any support or mentorship. Coupled with language challenges, it is of utmost importance to have a support group. We have our own small support groups at our universities. While Sainaa's work is mainly teaching in English with very little administrative work, I have to navigate through meetings, work reports, emails communicated mainly in Japanese. Sainaa's support group that consists of his peer faculties focuses on discussing teaching techniques and class or course management. My group consists of international female faculties, thus, we shared research works and supported each other personally and professionally. We have worked on various academic and administrative projects, providing language support to each other, reviewing research literature in English, Japanese, Chinese and Mongolian, and dividing our project tasks. Working together also helped us stay on track with publications and keep each other accountable.

As we reflect on our experiences as early career academics in Japan, we suggest the following strategies for those interested in academic jobs in Japan.

- *Job hunting process can be confusing in Japan, but academic jobs have a much flexible hiring process.* Academic jobs, particularly entry-level jobs such as researcher, fellow or assistant professor, can be very flexible compared to the corporate recruitment process. Universities trying to hire faculties with skills to work on the global landscape or in their international programs can be very flexible in terms of CV style or application material style. For example, while companies usually receive their applications by post, many jobs in academia receive their applications by email.

- *Start working in academia while in graduate school.* For those doing a graduate school in Japan, it is better to build their work profile while they are in graduate school. This includes writing for projects, building a professional network and working part-time in academia. We were able to receive job offers because we did few years of research and teaching assistant works.

- *Japanese language is important for tenure track jobs and promotion.* Although faculty jobs in internationally competitive programs would rather prioritize research background and possibility to produce cutting edge research outputs, most jobs, particularly in Social Sciences and Humanities, require Japanese skills. Although faculties have no problem communicating in English or other languages with other faculties and students, the administrative work language is usually Japanese. Therefore, tenure-track and long-term jobs usually require proficient Japanese skills. If you are interested in a long-term job in Japan, it is worth spending time learning the language.

- *Write as much as possible and publish.* Even if you do not have research funding, you need to continue your research. Otherwise, you will never get a research grant. I had started two separate research projects without any funding. One of them eventually received an external grant, and the other one secured a research assistant's grant from the university. If I had not started any project and waited until I received a grant, I would not have won any funding.

- *Build peer support group and support each other.* Peer support has been the most successful strategy for me to navigate the system without proficient Japanese language. While I supported my colleagues with English and research works, they supported me with the Japanese language. In addition, we provided support for one another as we negotiate our projects with other senior faculties and administrators. We hope this kind of early-career academic circle grows in our university.

During these last couple of years as early-career academics, we faced various challenges and experienced many opportunities to grow. The biggest obstacle for us has been the Japanese language. Although I have upper-intermediate Japanese level (and I still take Japanese language classes on Saturdays), it is still difficult to efficiently communicate at the academic and professional levels. The university has various support opportunities – however, we often do not know about them. Although universities welcome international faculties more than ever, most paper works and useful information is sent out in Japanese. If foreign faculties aim to stay in Japan for a long term, they need to develop a very good Japanese skill and build close connection with administrative and faculty groups.

Although we do not know how long we would stay in Japan, we will choose the scenario that works best for our professional and personal/family interest. I hope to complete my research grant and take my chances to pursue my career in Japan while Sainaa explores his career in Mongolia and in Japan.

REFERENCES

Green, D. (2019). Foreign faculty in Japan. *PS: Political Science & Politics*, 52(3), 523–526.

Huang, F. (2018). Foreign faculty at Japanese universities: Profiles and motivations. *Higher Education Quarterly*, 72(3), 237–249.

MEXT. (2017). Overview of ministry of education, culture, sports, science and technology. Retrieved from https://www.mext.go.jp/en/about/pablication/__icsFiles/afieldfile/2019/03/13/1374478_001.pdf

The Government of Japan. (2017). Points system aims to attract foreign talent to Japan. Retrieved from https://www.japan.go.jp/tomodachi/2017/summer2017/points_system_aims_to_attract.html

10

SHORT-TERM INTERNATIONAL MOBILITY AMONG ACADEMICS

Jisun Jung

ABSTRACT

Short-term international mobility has become popular among academics who are seeking new scholarly experiences abroad for a limited period. Short-term international mobility refers to staying abroad for a few days, weeks or months for scholarly work, although there is no specific definition of 'short'. In this chapter, I describe my experience of a five-month international stay on my first sabbatical. After positioning myself as a researcher on academic mobility and a mobile academic, I describe the international mobile experience from preparing to travel to returning home. Based on personal reflections, the chapter shares the challenges that early-career academics might confront and offers strategies to enjoy meaningful experiences in short-term mobility.

Keywords: Short-term mobility; sabbatical; international academics; early-career academics; academic networks; Australia

POSITIONING MYSELF AS A RESEARCHER ON ACADEMIC MOBILITY

As a researcher in higher education, I have studied international academic mobility for the last decade. I have been researching how internationalisation in higher education has affected international mobility among academics and how the impacts of mobility differ across academic generations in various higher education contexts (Jung, Kooij, & Teichler, 2013). My research has mainly involved East Asian higher education contexts, which have a high proportion of academics with international mobile experiences from their postgraduate studies, mainly involving English-speaking countries.

My research has investigated whether academics who have international mobile experiences outperform their peers without such experiences and whether itinerant academics have advantages over non-mobile academics in entering the academic job market (Jung, 2018; Shin, Jung, Postiglione, & Azman, 2014). To empirically demonstrate the impact of mobility experience, my studies have compared the scholarly output of mobile and non-mobile academics by controlling for other factors such as discipline and institution. Those studies have shown that mobility experiences positively affect academics' research output and entry positions. They also have long-term positive effects on research output, quality and visibility because they improve international research collaboration opportunities (Shin et al., 2014). However, those studies have also shown that these impacts vary by mobility duration, destination and academic field. Demographic backgrounds also matter; for example, female academics have fewer mobile experiences than male peers (Horta, Jung, & Santaos, 2019).

One of the challenges of researching academic mobility was defining the scope of international mobility, which has a wide variety of forms in terms of duration and purpose. Teichler (2015) broadly describes the international mobility of academics as a permanent form of 'migration' and temporary forms of 'mobility'. Some studies do not distinguish between migration and mobility, focussing instead on the duration of staying abroad – long term versus short term – and the purpose of staying; education versus work. Scholars have proposed different categorisations of international mobility such as early immigrants, doctoral immigrants, mobile study academics, doctoral mobile academics and professional migrants (Teichler, 2015).

Despite my theoretical and empirical research work on academic mobility, I realised a lack of self-reflection on how I have experienced different types of international mobility in my own academic career. Thus, in this chapter, I focus on my own international mobility experience and discuss the issues that might make such opportunities more meaningful and successful for others.

POSITIONING MYSELF AS A MOBILE ACADEMIC

One of the reasons I study academic mobility is my personal experience as a mobile academic. I was born in Korea, and my entire educational experience from early childhood through earning my doctoral degree was in that country. Before I began doctoral work, I was not keen to go abroad for further study. However, not long after I began that doctoral degree programme, I realised that having a doctoral degree from a highly esteemed overseas university would mean significant advantages in the academic job market in my country and could play a vital role in my long-term academic career progression. International mobility experience is regarded as a form of social and intellectual capital that distinguishes people from domestic degree holders (Kim, 2016).

To increase my academic portfolio as a domestic doctorate, I went to Hong Kong for a post-doctoral appointment. I initially made this decision because I wanted to include international working experience on my CV. Most mobile academics in East Asia are 'returnees,' meaning that they have long-term experiences studying for postgraduate degrees overseas and then returning to their home country, taking on academic positions to develop their academic careers. My case was different because I had a reverse mobile experience: studying at home and then working in another country. Based on previous studies, I can be identified as a 'professional migrant', 'international academic', 'foreign academic', 'expatriate' or 'long-stay post-doctorate', as I work in a country that is different from my nationality.

Even if I identify myself as an international mobile academic for my long-term career, my international mobile experience during study and work was not enough as my whole study experience was in my home country. Thus, I always tried to seek further mobility opportunities, even if they were only for the short term. Unlike long-term mobility for study or work, short-term mobility has not received substantial attention in higher education research. Short-term mobility refers to international stays that last from a couple of days to a few months, such as conference attendance, workshops, training, research visits or sabbaticals. As Henderson (2020) notes, short-term mobility is likely both to occur more frequently than longer-term mobility and to apply to more members of the academic profession.

A BRIEF DESCRIPTION OF MY SHORT-TERM
INTERNATIONAL MOBILITY

Although I have travelled more than 20 times to participate in international conferences since I started my career as an assistant professor, I had always been interested in spending more time at an overseas university to gain more international experience and situate myself in a new and inspiring academic environment. As soon as I became eligible to apply for sabbatical leave in my current rank, I looked for a potential place for my short-term visit. Under my current contract as an assistant professor, my sabbatical consists of six months of relief from teaching and other administrative tasks. Sabbatical leave allows academics to concentrate on specific scholarly activities by reducing their other duties. Academics take this period to devote themselves to write books and articles, collect data or learn new research methodologies. Academics are expected to return with new research ideas or outputs that enrich both their careers and their institutions.

Not all academics have the privilege of applying for sabbatical leave, which depends on whether an institution and faculty has enough resources to support a leave entitlement. Eligibility rules can vary across faculties, even within a single university. My faculties generously prioritise non-tenured assistant professors' sabbatical applications to support junior academics' efforts to focus on their research activities before they go through the competitive tenure and promotion evaluation process. Employers expect sabbatical leave will enhance a scholar's work upon his or her return; thus, they evaluate the applications using strict criteria that assess the goals and detailed plans of a sabbatical leave application.

I chose my destination for visits and wrote a proposal with detailed plans for six months of leave. Even after my faculty approved the application, I had to look for additional financial support to help me stay for several months in Melbourne, Australia, one of the world's most expensive cities. I was at the University of Melbourne for five months, from February to June 2019, on my first sabbatical. One could argue that sabbatical leave that covers more than a couple of months is not really short-term mobility. However, there is no specific time period that defines 'short' in the literature. I regard my five months of overseas stay as short-term mobility because it was a temporary research visit without any work contract; nor did it involve any visa issues.

The experience I relate in this chapter could be viewed as limited because the visit involved several months at an overseas institution, which is longer than typical short-term mobility. In addition, both my home and the host universities generously supported the entire process, from the cost to all administrative matters. Many academics, including myself, seek short-term international visits for different reasons that will expand their academic boundaries geographically and intellectually; however, not everyone can act quickly due to institutional and personal conditions. Some institutions do not have the financial resources to support your leave and temporarily hire someone to cover your workload. In particular, with today's financial constraints in many countries' higher education sectors, some international travel programmes may be eliminated or substantially reduced in scope. Even if your institution is willing to help with your international travel, there may still be barriers like family responsibilities to deciding to make the trip. Nevertheless, for those seeking short-term international travel, I would like to share some of my experiences in preparing for, staying at and returning from a mobile experience.

PREPARING

Find an opportunity. The first step in any international short-term mobility plan is to find an opportunity. The most common approach is to find a suitable institution and apply, as I did, for an internal sabbatical programme to take a leave of several months. Some of my colleagues have used global fellowship programmes that allow academics to conduct research outside their home country and negotiate with their home department to cover their absence. If you are away from campus for several months, there may be an extra burden on your colleagues, and you should allow plenty of time for discussions with your department chair and administrative staff to prepare and finalise a replacement plan. Again, in some institutions, this can be a more straightforward process than in others. You need to determine the policies your institution and department have regarding international travel by academic staff.

Find a funding opportunity. Finding available funding is another issue. You might need additional finance beyond your salary, or you might be on unpaid leave from your institution; in that case, you need to find funding sources to underwrite your visit. I was able to apply for university fellowship programmes that support international collaboration among academics at different universities. If no internal grants are available, governments and international agencies have funding programmes to support academic travel and research, although most of them are highly competitive.

Choose the right destination. One of the critical considerations in the short-term visit is deciding where to go. Besides specific destination-based programmes, such as exchanges between two institutions, academics have wide latitude in choosing their destinations. Academics have different priorities when choosing destinations, such as familiarity, geographic proximity, direct collaboration channels or institutional reputation. Some academics choose the places most familiar to them and largely maintain their academic routines, while others prefer a totally new environment and want to be far away from their everyday working routines. Some academics have more straightforward reasons than others in choosing a destination, such as data collection or archival research that must be carried out in specific locations. Some of my colleagues preferred to spend their sabbaticals in Hong Kong, because their research interests meant that they could collect data without leaving the city. When you have a collaborator or collaborators on a joint project, they may want you to visit them to maximise efficiency. Some prefer the destination where they earned their doctorate to renew their network of former colleagues, teachers and supervisors. Academics also compare the conditions of destinations, whether the potential host institutions provide substantial support and resources for visitors, and whether those institutions have the kind of reputation that will add value to an academic CV.

Finding a collaborator. Once you decide on your potential destination, finding a contact person in your host institution is crucial. Everything will be more accessible if you know someone at the host institution who can act as a gatekeeper and facilitator to help with your visit. Otherwise, you might have to contact someone in charge, such as the head of a research centre or department. It is also possible that nobody will reply to your email enquiries if you are dealing with a department where you do not have any acquaintances. I do not recommend persisting on a non-response, because the lack of a reply usually means that the department does not see any particular value in your visit. In such cases, you might have difficulty in developing a meaningful working relationship with colleagues at the host institution. The best strategy is to identify your research interests and strengths and contact someone who shares those interests about a potential collaboration. I was fortunate to have acquaintances with a few colleagues in the host institute through the long-term international research projects, and they were willing to host my visit. Their willingness were highly valuable to access the whole process. Developing networks during international conferences and meetings are always helpful when you search for the potential visiting institutes.

Have a clear goal to achieve. When I was planning my sabbatical in Melbourne, I wrote a proposal to apply for an internal grant. To improve my chances of obtaining funding, I asked a senior colleague to read my proposal and provide comments on whether it made sense. After reading my proposal, his first comment was, 'you have five months in Melbourne, and you can't do everything you wrote here. Five months are shorter than you think'. After receiving his comments, I realised that my proposal was far too ambitious for a five-month visit. It included several major research activities such as writing a journal article, crafting a research grant proposal, seeking collaborative opportunities and attending seminars at different universities. The proposal even had teaching plans such as observing classes in programmes similar to where I teach, seeking the opportunity to co-teach and developing a new course design. I also wrote that I was planning to interview academics and ask how they implemented their curricula in a programme like the one in my home department. People can have different purposes for international mobile experiences, especially when time is limited. It would be best if you had clear goals that are achievable and affordable. In the revised version of the proposal, I deleted the teaching plan and interview parts and restructured the proposal to focus only on research. Unless you have a specific project timeline to complete with colleagues at the host institution, you will likely have full autonomy to manage your time. What would your primary goal be for these few months? Do you want to have time to write while escaping from your office routine? Do you want to extend your network at host country institutions and promote your research? Do you want to find a new research collaborator? Do you want to have a variety of cultural experiences and improve your language proficiency?

Prepare as much as you can before leaving. Once you have a contact person at the host institution, it is better to prepare for your stay as much as you can before you leave. It would help if you let the contact person know when you will arrive and what help you might need. This could include everyday matters like receiving an invitation letter for your visa application (if one is needed), enquiring about university accommodations, obtaining office keys and gaining access to the host institution's computers and library facilities. To save time after your arrival, it is better to sort out such practical issues as early as possible. Some host institutions have plenty of experience with guest researchers and follow a protocol, but not all institutions have an established procedure to support your visit. If you plan to collect data in the host country or host institution, you may need to obtain research ethics approval in advance.

STAYING

Make routine your daily life. People have different reactions when they arrive in an unfamiliar place. Some adapt quickly to their new environment, while others need a couple of weeks to feel comfortable. When you arrive at your destination, you will need to figure out minor but essential issues of daily life like transportation, accommodation and getting used to the area. Give yourself some time to adapt, but do not take too long, as this is a short-term visit. Creating a routine is vital to maintaining a working rhythm.

Keep your expectations in check. Although I had narrowed down my goals before I boarded my flight to Melbourne for a five-month trip, I still had high hopes for what I could accomplish: finishing incomplete papers, writing a grant proposal, speaking with new people, giving seminars at other universities, weekend excursions and flying to other cities in Australia. As you might have guessed, achieving all those goals was impossible. It is essential to check your expectations and goals regularly and make detailed plans to achieve those aims. I regret that I focussed too much on the research I usually do, meeting deadlines I had and writing papers that I had already started. Take some new and risky approaches that you can only explore when you are in a new academic environment. I had several opportunities to attend the seminars and workshops given by the host institute. Some of them gave fresh research ideas and motivated me to apply similar approaches in my context. Although I could not transform those ideas into concrete actions, it is vital to see different issues and think differently once you are in a new environment.

Participate in academic events at the host institution. Although my writing mainly involved research, I was already working on, I did my best to participate in different educational activities that my host institutions were organising. My host research centre had a full slate of research activities, including conferences, research seminars, research proposals by PhD students and guest speakers. I took advantage and explored the research they were conducting and how they were similar to or different from what my colleagues and students were doing. You might be surprised at how many people share their research interests even in another part of the world, and there are many things to share in both directions.

Do not expect people to approach you; take the initiative to interact with them. Unless you are already a well-known scholar, do not expect people to come and talk to you. Today's academics have hectic daily lives and do not have time to welcome every visitor that comes through the department. The research centre where I was located had weekly teas for centre members, and people were certainly friendly, including doctoral students, but not all host institutions have that kind of culture. Suppose you are allocated a private office and do not have an outgoing personality; in that case, you might go an entire day without a single conversation, and you might be there for months without really knowing anybody. Of course, there is nothing wrong with deciding to isolate yourself and concentrate on writing or primary research, but it is always better to acquaint yourself with new people as long as you are there.

Take the opportunity and reach out to people at universities in the same city. If you get to know the people at your host institutions, look around and see if more people might be interested in your research. Contact them, visit them, have seminars and promote your research. I managed to visit three other universities in Melbourne, attended academic events and held seminars for their faculty and students. These were great opportunities to extend my academic network and get to know some amazing colleagues.

How far would you like to be from your home institution? Some of my colleagues advised me to get as far away from my campus office routine as possible during my sabbatical and suggested I not even reply to most emails so that I could concentrate on my research. Of course, this is impossible, particularly if you supervise postgraduate students and are engaged in plans for the upcoming academic years. One strategy is to create a boundary in terms of time availability and set up an automatic email reply so that people are aware of when you are available for immediate communication.

If you have left family behind, talk to them as much as you can. It can be difficult for some academics to leave their families behind, especially if young children are involved. Henderson (2020) uses the concept of 'sticky care' to describe how international mobility brings out the challenges a family's critical carer when having to leave home, even for a couple of days. Research on gender issues in the academic profession highlights the unequal challenges that women face in engaging in a mobile academic career. When I went to Melbourne, my two children were three years and one year old. People always had the same reaction when they learned I was on my own: 'Wow, you left your young kids in Hong Kong? They must miss you so much!' Yes, they did, and I missed them too, so I had to endure some guilt feelings when I had those reactions from people. Sometimes, you have the time to do something for your career and need to take action. As long as you maintain daily communication, things should work out fine.

RETURNING

Acknowledge the host and maintain your network. If you enjoyed your time away, do not forget to thank your host institution and tell your newfound colleagues how much you enjoyed your stay and appreciated their hospitality. Even if there are no direct collaboration opportunities in the short term, there might be opportunities to work with them in the future. It is always essential to maintain your network and keep the people you have met updated about your latest research efforts.

Reflect on your experience and make a long-term research plan. Your funding agency will likely require you to submit a report of your activities. You might summarise what you did for a few months and be surprised at how much (or how little!) you did during the visit. I recall once reading some advice that the point of visiting other universities for a few months is not only to increase your short-term output but also to make long-term research plans. Today's early-career academics are surrounded by deadlines, publications and demands for output. Still, a mobility experience in a new academic environment should provide you with time to reflect on the research plan you might want to focus on in the next stage of your academic career.

CONCLUSION

Being in a new academic environment provides the time to assess your scholarly works and an opportunity to re-evaluate your career goals. Thus, short-term international mobility is a valuable experience for many academics, although several professional and personal issues should be considered before decision-making. There might be, of course, some constraints and obstacles to have the ideal type of short-term mobility with individual and institutional conditions. To improve the chance of meaning short-term mobility experience, in this chapter, I explored the meaning of mobility as an early-career academic and shared the five months of my first sabbatical experience in an overseas university. The experience was described as three stages; preparing, staying and returning. For instance, in the preparation stage, I emphasised the importance of finding a suitable opportunity, destination and financial support. The more you are prepared, the better experience you would get. In addition, it is essential to maintain and check your goals during the stay. Finally, it is advisable to acknowledge both home and host institutions and reflecting yourself and your long-term scholarly goals after returning.

REFERENCES

Henderson, E. F. (2020). Sticky care and conference travel: Unpacking care as an explanatory factor for gendered academic immobility. *Higher Education.* doi:10.1007/s10734-020-00550-1

Horta, H., Jung, J., & Santaos, J. M. (2019). Mobilities impact on current research output, quality, and visibility of academics in city-based higher education systems. *Higher Education Policy, 33*(3), 437–458. doi:10.1057/s41307-019-00173-x

Jung, J. (2018). Domestic and overseas doctorates and their academic job entries in South Korea. *Asian Education and Development Studies, 7*(2), 205–222.

Jung, J., Kooij, R., & Teichler, U. (2013). Internationalization and the new generation of academics. In M. Finkelstein, F. Huang, & M. Rostan (Eds.), *The internationalization of the academy: Changes, realities and prospects* (pp. 207–236). Cham: Springer.

Kim, J. (2016). Global cultural capital and global positional competition: International graduate students' transnational occupational trajectories. *British Journal of Sociology of Education, 37*(1), 30–50. doi:10.1080/01425692.2015.1096189

Shin, J. C., Jung, J., Postiglione, G. A., & Azman, Z. (2014). Research productivity of returnees from study abroad in Korea, Hong Kong, and Malaysia. *Minerva*, *52*(4), 467–487. doi:10.1007/s11024-014-9259-9

Teichler, U. (2015). Academic mobility and migration: What we know and what we do not know. *European Review*, *23*(S1), S6–S37. doi:10.1017/S1062798714000787

11

INTERNATIONAL ACADEMIC MOBILITY: CATEGORIES OF DIFFERENCE AND NARRATIVES OF POSSIBILITY

James Burford and Mary Eppolite

ABSTRACT

In this chapter, we explore our academic mobility journeys – with particular consideration of the role of gender, class and sexual identity. The chapter takes shape as a dialogue, where together, we discuss the challenges and opportunities we encountered, the strategies we enacted and the successes we have had as scholars on the move. By having a conversation with an-Other about our mobile subjectivities, we hope to offer points of reflection for other international academics as they contemplate or negotiate their own movements.

Keywords: Academic mobility; gender; sexuality; queer; Thailand; women

INTRODUCTION

This is a chapter that explores the social identities of international academics. We offer narratives of possibility for migrant academics who, by virtue of their gender, class background or sexual identity, may experience exclusion and marginality in the international higher education (IHE) workforce. As academic mobility researchers ourselves, we understand that there are many 'hidden narratives' that surround academic migration, particularly regarding the uneven distribution of opportunities 'among different social groups and geopolitical spaces' (Morley, Alexiadou, Garaz, González-Monteagudo, & Taba, 2018, p. 537). For example, Manzi, Ojeda, and Hawkins (2019) argue that 'mobility…is often predicated on the premise of an existing ideal male, white and heterosexual subject' (p. 357). We, the two authors of this chapter, disrupt some of these ideals and reproduce others. We are James (a middle-class Pākehā queer academic from Aotearoa (New Zealand), who is in his mid-30s) and Mary (a working-class white American heterosexual cis-woman, who is in her late 20s).[1] We worked together at the same education faculty in Thailand, meeting when James was sitting on a panel interviewing prospective candidates, and Mary was the successful applicant. We have subsequently gone on to collaborate on a project which explored the experiences of academic migrants working in Thailand (see Burford, Eppolite, Koompraphant, & Uerpairojkit, 2021; Burford, Uerpairojkit, Eppolite, & Vachananda, 2019). While Thailand is Mary's first destination as an international academic, James has also worked in Australia and is in the process of relocating to the United Kingdom as we finish writing this chapter.

In order to produce this chapter, we engaged in a project of reading across studies that consider how academic mobilities may be connected to questions of identity and social inequities. We searched for literature that considers the international mobility experiences across intersecting categories of difference, including for queer academics, working-class academics, and academic women. Once we had read and discussed this research together, we recorded a conversation focused on our journeys and how our own identities shaped our experiences as international academics and vice versa. When we had a transcript of this conversation on the page, we collaboratively edited it into its present form.

A CONVERSATION BETWEEN TWO INTERNATIONAL ACADEMICS

Mary: I'm looking forward to speaking to you, Jamie. Can you tell me about how you came to be an international academic?

Jamie: Oh, that's a complicated question! It's hard to know how far back to go to answer it. I guess I've always been interested in living overseas. I grew up in a rural area outside of Christchurch in New Zealand. And from an early age I knew that I wanted to live somewhere else. I think part of this was about realising I was queer and not really seeing how to make a life for myself in my hometown, where the expectations surrounding what young men might do seemed really fixed and non-negotiable.[2] So that's one answer; I developed an orientation to being somewhere other than 'home'. I think in addition to this, I was exposed to travel early within my family, as my Mum was a part-time academic and took a number of short visiting academic positions in Malaysia, once bringing our family along with her. So, I had the example of someone close to me who had also been an international academic. After graduating with my B.A. in 2006, I spent a year in Taiwan teaching English and learning Mandarin, and then returned to New Zealand to do my master's degree in 2008. During my master's, I undertook five months of field research in Bangkok. While I was in Bangkok, I developed a relationship and then returned to New Zealand with my former Thai partner, who went on to do his PhD. So, it is via this relationship and my Master's fieldwork that my ongoing connection to Thailand really began. In 2013, once my partner had finished his PhD, and while I was in the middle of my own PhD, we decided to return to Thailand so he could take up an academic position. Because Thai immigration did not recognise same-sex relationships, I needed to find a position in Thailand in order to join him. Fortunately, I was offered a visiting fellowship at Mahidol University, where my partner was working at the time. While I spent most of my time there finishing my PhD, I also joined the wider community of the centre, teaching the occasional class and joining a research project.

Mary: It sounds like you had experiences with academic mobility from an early age. I know before leaving New Zealand, you were working in the area of LGBTQI+ community development. I'm curious, if you stayed in New Zealand, do you think you would have taken the leap into academic work? It seems like you fell into working at a university as a result of your relationship at the time.

Jamie: I think I was probably already moving in an academic direction. I'd worked on campus at a student union, and had tutored various subjects, and was already part-way through my PhD. So, I think academia was something I was hoping to head towards, but accompanying my partner accelerated things.

Mary: So, you were a visiting scholar at Mahidol for about a year and a half, while finishing your PhD in education at Auckland by distance. How did you get to Thammasat, where we met?

Jamie: While I was at Mahidol, I learned that three of my colleagues had been approached to found a new faculty of Learning Sciences and Education at Thammasat University. They were searching for another colleague to join the team and invited me in. I was significantly more junior than them, but I could see it was an amazing opportunity. When else might I get to be a part of developing a new faculty like this? So, I said yes.

Mary: Why do you think you were offered this position? Do you think that it has anything to do with the fact that you were an international candidate?

Jamie: It's difficult to know without asking, but I do think it mattered, yes. While I had worked with my colleagues previously, and they knew what I could bring to this project, part of what we were trying to do in founding this new faculty was to energise some different ways of thinking about learning and education in Thailand. Teacher training in Thailand is a conservative and highly regulated area, and we wanted to push the boundaries of what might be possible. However, I think the fact that I was a foreigner and could be hired on a 'Foreign Expert' contract was helpful institutionally, as was the fact that I was already writing and publishing early on in my PhD, which is something that my colleagues thought was valuable. The fact that I am a white man who was working in Thailand cannot be left to recede to the background, however. Across lots of research on educational migration in Thailand (e.g. Ferguson, 2008; Hickey, 2018) you'll see that there is significant privilege accorded to white migrants. I think I was a recipient of that privilege. There is also the question of nationality. Myself as a New Zealander and you an American, we both have passports that are easier to travel on. This is not a privilege shared by all academic migrants hoping to work in Thailand.

Mary: That's a really important point to think about how race, nationality, and gender shape our capacities to be mobile.

Jamie: How about you Mary? Could you tell me a little more about your journey towards becoming an international academic?

Mary: I guess my journey into academic work feels a little roundabout. I come from a low-income background, but thankfully had great educational opportunities and mentors to support me along the way. I often tell people that if it weren't for them, I wouldn't be in the place I am today. When I started at university, my plan was to go into teaching and inspire students like myself. But I decided I wanted to be an academic when I became a Ronald E. McNair Post-baccalaureate Scholar.[3] For two years, the McNair program and mentors provided training in research, academic procedures, provided funding opportunities and GRE prep classes, and organised graduate school tours. We even learned about the small, often forgotten details, like how to dress for conferences presentations.

At my university, professors received a list of qualifying students who were able to apply to the programme. My French advisor noticed I was on the list and invited me to apply with her as my project mentor. We had just returned to Wisconsin from a short immersion programme in Louisiana studying Cajun culture and she wanted to know if I would be interested in researching linguistic variation in Louisiana French. As I recall, our initial meeting to talk about the application was a little awkward. I had never heard of this programme, let alone considered getting a PhD before. I had spent the majority of my life dreaming of being a classroom teacher. I was reluctant to apply, and at the time, I was well on my way to pursuing a degree in elementary education. However, my nominating advisor encouraged me to consider that *teaching* could be imagined in different ways. That led to me shifting my career path.

I liked learning and teaching and thought academia could be a lot of fun. Part of the challenge I faced was renegotiating my identity as a teacher, which took time. Ultimately, I decided to defer graduate school (which was not encouraged by the programme) and instead went to teach English in France for a year. When I informed the McNair programme director of my plan to take a gap year, she jokingly told me that I 'never followed the traditional path, why would I start now?' Since then, I've been able to work in various language programmes around the world and now at universities in Thailand.

Jamie: It's so interesting to hear more about your story into academic work. Could you tell me about your journey to Thailand?

Mary: So, my master's was in teaching English to speakers of other languages. I studied at a small internationally focused private graduate school; we only had about 115 students on campus. The curriculum is built on alternative pedagogies of teaching and learning, a little hippy-dippy. We even had our own yurt on campus! My time there nudged me further towards an international mindset. At the end of my studies, I started looking for positions in the English Language field that might be closer to the part of the world where my partner at the time was working. Ideally, I was looking for a role that involved teaching, curriculum design, and research. That's a tall order to find! But a professor, who was helping me look for my next opportunity, saw the Thai position advertised and emailed me. It's just one of those things; I looked over the application and knew 'oh crap' this was going to be my job. It just gave me the right feeling. It wasn't that I wanted to go to Thailand in particular. The job was giving me opportunities that I wanted, and I thought 'we'll see what happens', which has really been a theme of a lot of my global mobility.

Jamie: It sounds like your story has had a lot of serendipity, but also you have had important mentors who have guided you and thrown opportunities in your direction.

Mary: There have been a lot of wonderful people along the way. Learning the ins and outs of academic culture has not been simple. I'm a first-generation university student, so I've often been on my own when it came to figuring out how to apply to university or for financial aid. The mentors I've encountered have been instrumental in providing that knowledge to overcome challenges. Jamie, I'm curious, have you faced any barriers in your journey as an international academic?

Jamie: Yes, there have been barriers. I think the first one surrounds linguistic and cultural adaptation in Thailand. While there are often similarities about 'ideas' of the university around the world, these are also often grounded in local interpretations of questions like: How do we teach? How should we be with each other as academics? What is the role of an academic in relation to students and society? I had to learn and unlearn a lot when I moved to Thailand as I tried to answer some of these questions. Other barriers I encountered were around language. I didn't speak Thai fluently when I arrived and learning Thai is still a work in progress for me. All of the departments I worked at in Thailand have had members of staff who can speak English but have mostly been predominantly Thai-language settings. That's been a barrier to my participation. But I've always had supportive colleagues and found ways of being kept in the loop. It's also been a good opportunity to develop my Thai language abilities. However, I want to say that cultural adaptation isn't just a barrier. I am *interested* in Thailand and Thai IHE, so I was *interested* in what it means to be an academic in Thailand. Sometimes I've made mistakes or held assumptions that have been challenged, and my Thai colleagues have done this with significant generosity.

Mary: Yes – that echoes with my experience too. It's also interesting to hear that something which could be presented as a barrier is also an opportunity for learning and growth.

Jamie: Yeah, that's right, I think many aspects of academic mobility have these double edges, don't they?

Mary: Totally. Were there any other barriers that you'd like to share?

Jamie: Well, I suppose another barrier relates to Thailand's place in the global IHE economy, which meant that some of the resources that I could take for granted in New Zealand weren't available in Thailand. For example, the salary I had in Thailand was lower than that which I might have received at home, which ultimately was a barrier to staying in Thailand for long term. There were also differences with regard to funding opportunities, including research and conferences, as well as other things like library subscriptions and access to facilities. This has a material impact on academic work. But there is also a symbolic effect of Thailand's position in the IHE economy. I struggled for some time with the limits of my own academic recognisability. It seemed that when I was talking to colleagues overseas, at a conference, for example, they couldn't recognise my experience in Thailand as equivalent to the kinds of work done by a scholar in the Global North. It was as if my movement to Thailand was somehow unusual and potentially career-limiting. It took a while for me to be able to have these conversations and really articulate the opportunities that academic work in Thailand was offering me.

I guess a final barrier I'll talk about is that my romantic relationships have not been legally recognised in Thailand. This has meant that I've been dependent on having a job for my immigration status, despite being in two long-term relationships while I was living there. But in terms of being queer in Thailand, on the whole, I found much that was really fulfilling. I did not experience the same level of street harassment and homophobia I have in other places I've lived (although my own experiences here may not be shared by others), and I found a niche within Thai universities to conduct queer research. I guess I want to say that my sexuality has been both a barrier in terms of immigration, but also a significant source of possibility and connection with colleagues and in terms of the agendas. It has opened up for my scholarship.

Mary: Yeah, I know we have talked about this in the past. There are some similarities between what you mentioned and my own experience with cultural and language adjustment.

Jamie: I am wondering if you also experience the barriers of recognition that I mentioned, given that your area of scholarship is teaching English as a second language?

Mary: I do feel some of those same issues around recognition. With my background in teaching English, I am particularly aware of the colonial legacy that English teachers bring with them when they are mobile and how that legacy continues in this field. I also think about the 'seriousness' of being an English teacher, particularly in a context where backpacker teachers may be recognised in ways that are similar to me (see Eppolite & Burford, 2020). This is compounded by the fact that I am a woman because the applicant pool here is very masculine, and white in particular. I acknowledge that I benefit from the privileges of being white here in Thailand.[4] But as a woman, I have had a number of uncomfortable conversations with male academic colleagues, crediting my gender as the reason I have been offered particular roles as an academic. It's really frustrating to hear that a career you've dedicated your life to, and care deeply about, can be reduced to: 'you're just a woman, that's why you've got this job'. I avoid some professional gatherings because I don't want to encounter those kinds of comments. Luckily, within my department now there are a number of international academic women, which has enabled me to nurture some important friendships and has given me a greater sense of community.

Jamie: I think this 'you're just...' kind of talk exemplifies how international academic women can be positioned as marginal in the field in Thailand. There are some other gender questions circulating in the field, particularly surrounding the 'mobility imperative' in academia. This is the idea that going abroad as an academic is essential for developing a strong academic career. When we look across the literature, a number of scholars examined the structural patterning of international academic mobility, with a particular focus on gender inequalities (see Leemann, 2010; Pettersson, 2011). Increasingly, researchers have identified that women academics may be less likely to be mobile than men. We might want to ask some tough questions about the binary ways gender is often constructed in this field because the world is not only made up of people who identify as men and women. However, I still think these studies offer some important insights. I'm wondering what you make of this research and how it connects to your own mobility narrative?

Mary: You're right. Research has shown that women academics tend to be less geographically mobile than men, or have particular mobility patterns. Some of the constraints on women's academic mobility relate to family obligations (Leeman, 2010). However, this hasn't been the case for me, as someone who does not have children. This isn't without contest though; my mom often asks me when I plan on moving home and 'starting a family'. My parents see academia as a risk. It's hard to share my academic success, like papers being accepted or conference presentations with them. They are proud of me, but I think they understand success more in terms of the size of a pay cheque. Not because they are financially motivated, but they want me to have savings and retirement. Currently, those opportunities feel more limited as a mobile academic. At this point in my life, I have chosen not to think about the difficulties of combining international academic mobility and a dual-career relationship!

Jamie: Ah yes, this is slightly different from me. My partner is finishing his PhD and he'll be moving alongside me shortly. In fact, just last night, we were watching videos of the place we might be moving to in the next couple of months once I start my new job in the United Kingdom! Mary, I want to switch directions a little now. You've spoken about some barriers, how about the opportunities that you have found being an international academic?

Mary: I've had a number of great opportunities in Thailand. Luckily with the demonstration school in its early stages of development, I was able to be creative with curriculum design. Since the school was affiliated with the faculty, I also had the chance to participate in research and build a small network of colleagues. Both institutions I've worked for have been mindful about hiring quality candidates, including those outside the typical applicant pool. It's paradoxical: on the one hand, I acknowledge that hiring committees may be looking for diversity in academia, but on the other, I am nervous others will interpret my success as 'easy'. I have a full-time academic position, and since I hold a Master's degree rather than a PhD, I know it would be almost impossible for me to find an equivalent position at home in the United States. How about you, Jamie? What opportunities have you found coming out of your experience as an international academic?

Jamie: For a few years, I worried that it was going to be difficult for me to make progress in my academic career, and I was actively looking for jobs for some time. Eventually, I was offered a role in Australia, and I have now found that my experience in both Thailand and Australia is being seen as an asset. This is even more true as I look to my next international academic move to the United Kingdom, where I will be teaching Global Education and International Development. My experience in Thailand and my research agenda that I began there is, I imagine, a factor in getting this job. My experience in Thailand has also significantly shaped my identity as a researcher. Much of my research is now about Thai IHE, and this would not be something I would have researched had I not moved there. When I talk about my teacher identity, I often say that I became an *aa-jaan* (academic) in Thailand. I was mentored by exceptional educators and had the luxury of spending my first three years co-teaching. I've also been lucky to learn about indigenous Thai pedagogies and was fortunate to be able to take on leadership roles very early in my career. So now, when I enter the job market, I can speak to these experiences. I'm not sure I would have had all of these opportunities had I not moved to Thailand.

Mary: It sounds like you have been able to embrace a number of opportunities! As you know, international academic mobility is often identified as a strategy for getting ahead in academia and is often associated with quality and excellence (Leeman, 2010). Did you have a longer-term plan or overall aim?

Jamie: I wouldn't say I had an overall strategy when I arrived in Thailand and started working as an academic. I think that I developed a plan as I went along. After a few years of working in universities and once I finished my PhD, I had a sense that I wanted to move back closer to home and set about trying to find my next position. I'm not sure I thought about it particularly strategically, but I was involved in a number of international networks and research collaborations and had service roles in my field. All of these brought me into contact with other researchers, and I let them know I was on the job market. They helped with channelling opportunities in my direction. Again, I'm not sure I thought about it as a strategy, but I grounded my research in Thailand while I was in Thailand. And I have always enjoyed the writing and publishing side of academic work. I wouldn't say I have the most planned-out career, but as I reflect back on it, I have been working in a number of related areas and chasing around a couple of questions that capture my imagination. But I certainly didn't set out to be the idealised academic 'entrepreneur', which Leeman (2010) describes as 'nomadic and monadic...de-territorialised, disembodied and dis-embedded' (p. 619). I have been very interested in the place I live and how I live there, the connections I develop, and the accountabilities I have where I am. That being said, I guess I can recognise my upcoming movement as part of the hypermobility desired within the contemporary academic profession (Manzi et al., 2019). Since I graduated with my doctorate around four years ago, this will be the third country I've worked in as an academic.

Mary: I have been similar with my unplanned career path. My plan has been to 'say yes to opportunities'. It sounds strange to say that I 'ended up' in Thailand but I just kind of ended up here. However, I am trying to use it to my advantage. I hope I'll be able to take these experiences to be a competitive PhD candidate, which is my overall goal.

Jamie: It sounds like neither of us were particularly strategic in thinking through some of our mobility decisions! But we have both developed plans since we've arrived and tried to make the most of the opportunities that are available to us. I am wondering if you could identify a couple of successes that you have experienced as an international academic in Thailand?

Mary: What do you think success means? I think many of the things we've talked about today could be seen in this way.

Jamie: I think this is up to us to define what success looks like. I think it would be cool to hear what success as an 'international academic' looks like and means for you?

Mary: I think what makes this question challenging is that sometimes successes might feel like failures. In being mobile academics, we balance a lot of mixed feelings. I have been given fantastic opportunities via mobility, but I also need to acknowledge that these have sometimes left me feeling isolated and overwhelmed. I also think it's important to wrestle with those ethical questions that any mobile academic should ask themselves about where we are coming from and where we land, and the kinds of privileges we experience. With that being said, I don't know if I can define myself as successful until I've actually left here and continued onto graduate school. It's hard to compare myself to my contemporaries from my Master's programme, some of whom are just finishing their PhDs now and searching for academic jobs. Technically, the McNair programme will consider me to have 'failed', because I won't have finished my PhD within 10 years of finishing my undergraduate degree. Even though you and I have been trying to deconstruct ideas like 'backwards mobility' in our collaborative work, I still sometimes find myself 'looking North' and comparing myself to others. So, I don't think I have failed; I think that I am just taking a scenic route towards academia! I think moving a little more slowly has been a way for me to acclimatise myself to what can sometimes feel like a pretty alien environment. I think being an international academic in Thailand has offered me an opportunity to come to academia more on my own terms, and hopefully, if this experiment is successful, I'll go forward using the knowledge that I have gained. What about you Jamie?

Jamie: In New Zealand we have a saying that the kūmara (sweet potato) does not speak of its own sweetness. So, this is an uncomfortable question to try and answer! I've also learned from some wonderful academic mentors (e.g. Grant, 2019; Khoo, 2018) to query the terms by which academic success is commonly defined. I think some of the things I've been successful at in my career are building relationships based on mutual learning, working across cultures with respect and working across disciplinary boundaries with genuine curiosity. I guess I've been open to different ways of working and different types of projects. Some people might see this as a strategy; I think I've just been more driven by joy in thinking with other people and the excitement of embarking on a new knowledge project. So, this also means that any success that I've had is shared with my colleagues. I guess by some standards, I've had a productive career so far in terms of the kinds of things institutions tend to 'count'. But what I'm more interested in is the work I've been able to do and the people I've been able to do it with. I can certainly say that being an international academic has stretched my thinking beyond what I might have even imagined was possible.

CONCLUSION

In this short dialogue, we have shared our experiences of becoming international academics. We wrote this chapter because we feel that many representations of academic mobility, which present it as a line in a CV or a movement on a map, risk tidying it up and minimising its complexity. It was our hope to give a more 'lived' sense of what being an international academic can look and feel like. We hope that our conversation resonates with other international academics, whether you see yourself in aspects of our story or have a different experience.

The narratives we share in the chapter reveal that the impetus for academic mobility and our orientation to the academy were dissimilar, with one of us having a clearer 'map' to aspire in its direction. And yet, we both benefit from privilege accorded to our whiteness, our nationalities, and our language backgrounds. A key theme that emerged through both of our stories was the importance of networks and mentors (formal and informal), who played key roles in assisting us in making important education and career transitions.

In this chapter we also reflect on elements of our social identities, as a queer man, and a working-class woman. As we noted at the outset of this chapter, the global higher education sector tends to reproduce wider social inequalities that surround race, class, gender, sexuality, among others. In this chapter, we share our stories for others who may sit uneasily in relation to academic mobility norms. We wanted to share narratives of possibility because, despite the turbulence that inevitably accompanies mobility, we have found that there are rich possibilities and pleasures too.

NOTES

1. A Māori term for people of non-Māori descent, typically of European origins.
2. Other scholars of academic mobility have also considered the connections between their academic mobility and their desires to survive, or indeed escape homophobia and heteronormativity (see Blanco & Saunders, 2019, p. 668).
3. The McNair Scholar Programme is a federally funded US initiative to train qualifying undergraduate students for doctoral studies.
4. A number of migrant educators of colour have written about experiences with racism in Thai educational institutions (e.g. Kris WYA, 2017; Perez-Amurao & Sunanta, 2020).

REFERENCES

Blanco, G. L., & Saunders, D. B. (2019). Giving account of our (mobile)selves: Embodied and relational notions of academic privilege in the international classroom. *Teaching in Higher Education*, *24*(5), 666–677. doi:10.1080/13562517.2019.1621281

Burford, J., Eppolite, M., Koompraphant, G., & Uerpairojkit, T. (2021). Narratives of 'stuckness' among North–South academic migrants in Thailand: Interrogating normative logics and global power asymmetries of transnational academic migration. *Higher Education*. doi:10.1007/s10734-020-00672-6

Burford, J., Uerpairojkit, T., Eppolite, M., & Vachananda, T. (2019). Analysing the national and institutional policy landscape for foreign academics in Thailand: Opportunity, ambivalence and threat. *Journal of Higher Education Policy and Management*, *41*(4), 416–429. doi:10.1080/1360080X.2019.1606881

Eppolite, M., & Burford, J. (2020). Producing un/professional academics: Category boundary work among migrant academics in Thai higher education. *Globalisation, Societies and Education*, *18*(5), 528–540. doi:10.1080/14767724.2020.1805300

Ferguson, M. (2008). *Becoming ajarn: A narrative inquiry into stories of teaching and livingabroad*. Unpublished Master's Thesis. Canada: University of Victoria.

Grant, B. M. (2019). Wrestling with career: An autoethnographic tale of a cracked academic self. In D. Bottrell & C. Manathunga (Eds.). *Resisting neoliberalism in higher education* (Vol. I, pp. 119–134). Palgrave. doi:10.1007/978-3-319-95942-9_6

Hickey, M. (2018). Thailand's 'English fever', migrant teachers and cosmopolitan aspirations in an interconnected Asia. *Discourse: Studies in the Cultural Politics of Education*, 39(5), 738–751. doi:10.1080/01596306.2018.1435603

Khoo, T. (2018). The right kind of ambition. In N. Lemon & S. McDonough (Eds.), *Mindfulnessin the academy: Practices and perspectives from scholars* (pp. 233–244). Springer.

Kris WYA. (2017, July 7). Teaching in Thailand…While Black. [Blog post]. Retrieved from https://kriswya.wordpress.com/2017/07/07/teaching-in-thailand-while-black/

Leemann, R. J. (2010). Gender inequalities in transnational academic mobility and the ideal type of academic entrepreneur. *Discourse: Studies in the Cultural Politics of Education*, 31(5), 605–625. doi:10.1080/01596306.2010.516942

Manzi, M., Ojeda, D., & Hawkins, R. (2019). "Enough wandering around!": Life trajectories, mobility, and place making in neoliberal academia. *The Professional Geographer*, 71(2), 355–365. doi:10.1080/00330124.2018.1531036

Morley, L., Alexiadou, N., Garaz, S., González-Monteagudo, J., & Taba, M. (2018). Internationalisation and migrant academics: The hidden narratives of mobility. *Higher Education*, 76(3), 537–554. doi:10.1007/s10734-017-0224-z

Perez-Amurao, A. L., & Sunanta, S. (2020). They are 'Asians just like us': Filipino teachers, colonial aesthetics and English language education in Thailand. *Sojourn: Journal of Social Issues in Southeast Asia*, 35(1), 108–137. Retrieved from https://www.jstor.org/stable/26883617

Pettersson, H. (2011). Gender and transnational plant scientists: Negotiating academic mobility, career commitments and private life. *GENDER – Zeitschrift für Geschlecht, Kultur und Gesellschaft*, 3(1), 99–116. Retrieved from https://nbn-resolving.org/Urn:nbn:de:0168-ssoar-394570

INDEX